Sheet
Pan
Magic

Sue Quinn

Sheet Pan Magic

One pan, one meal, no fuss!

Photography by Faith Mason

quadrille

Publishing Director: Sarah Lavelle
Creative Director: Helen Lewis
Commissioning Editor: Céline Hughes
Designer: Gemma Hayden
Design Assistant: Shani Travers
Photography: Faith Mason
Prop Stylist: Luis Peral
Food Stylist: Rosie Reynolds
Food Stylist Assistant: Jess Dennison
Production Controller: Nikolaus Ginelli
Production Director: Vincent Smith

First published in 2017 by
Quadrille Publishing Limited
Pentagon House
52–54 Southwark Street
London SE1 1UN
www.quadrille.com

Quadrille is an imprint of Hardie Grant
www.hardiegrant.com

Cataloguing in Publication Data: a catalogue record for this book
is available from the British Library.

ISBN: 978 1 78713 048 7

Printed in China

Contents

Introduction

There's no getting away from the fact that cooking often involves a little bit of drudgery. Complicated recipes to follow, multiple pots to stir and mountains of dishes to wash can make cooking seem like hard graft, especially on weeknights when time is short and people just want to eat. There's a place for complicated dishes, of course, but even enthusiastic home cooks often want food that is simple to make, delicious to eat and doesn't entail using every pot in the kitchen. So, for those who haven't fallen under the spell of sheet pan magic before, this book might well be a revelation.

Every recipe within these pages—snacks, appetizers, complete meals, warm salads and desserts—requires just one sheet pan to make. Such a surprisingly wide range of dishes emphasizes just how underrated this humble piece of kitchen equipment is. But sheet pan cooking does more than just smooth the culinary path when your cooking mojo is low and demand for a tasty meal is high; it also delivers food that is especially delicious.

Why don't sheet pans play a more prominent role in everyday home cooking? As it turns out, the concept is relatively new. As food historian Bee Wilson explains in her book *Consider the Fork: A History of How We Cook and Eat*, for hundreds of years chefs in European kitchens considered ovens to be suitable only for baking things like bread. Meat and game, meanwhile, were roasted over an open flame.

According to Wilson, this division continued until the early twentieth century, which goes some way to explain why stovetops have been the default method for cooking vegetables and smaller cuts of meat until relatively recently.

Restaurant chefs are now well versed in the benefits of sheet pan cooking; stick your head around the door of a professional kitchen and you're likely to see all manner of foods going into the oven in pans, from fillets of fish to vegetables. Chefs use this technique because it simplifies the cooking process and delivers wonderfully tasty results. Home cooks have been a little slower to catch on to the benefits; in domestic kitchens, sheet pans are still most strongly associated with cakes and joints of meat—food that doesn't readily cook on the stovetop. Hopefully this book will help change that.

Food roasted in the oven is not only convenient, but also especially flavorsome. During roasting, dry heat wraps itself around the food, locking in and concentrating flavors. At a high heat, roasted food turns gloriously burnished because the natural sugars caramelize on the outside, sealing in the juices on the inside.

Make friends with your sheet pan

All the recipes in this book have been developed and tested in a rectangular **sheet pan measuring 8 x 12 x 2in.** For some of the snacky dishes, such as chicken scratchings, sausage rolls, corn fritters, whole Camembert and the like, the size of the pan isn't crucial, so long as the food isn't crowded together (in which case it will steam). For dishes where the food fills the pan to a particular height, like porridge, brownies, bread rolls and cake, it's important to use the recommended size, otherwise they might not cook successfully, and/or in the specified time. For dishes such as Chicken Thighs with Creamy Leek and Caper Sauce (on page 117) it's best to use the recommended pan size; something larger, for example, could see the sauce spread too thin and burn.

In fact, if you want to make the most of this book, it would be a good idea to invest in a sheet pan of the recommended size. It won't accommodate an enormous Thanksgiving turkey, obviously, but how often do you use a sheet pan that large? What you will have, though, is a single piece of versatile kitchen equipment that's ideal for cooking a wide range of dishes, from cakes to joints of meat.

If you're shopping for a new sheet pan, use the same rule that applies for cake pans and baking sheets: opt for something solid and the best quality that you can afford. Steel/stainless steel (or multi-layered stainless steel and aluminum), anodized aluminum and cast iron are popular choices; or, if you want to break the bank, copper is wonderful. A heavier pan resists warping and distributes the heat more evenly, so your cooking results will be better overall. And make sure you're buying the right size: the measurements previously mentioned refer to the inside measurements of the pan.

Go for a sheet pan with rounded corners for easy cleaning, as well as handles for safely transferring it in and out of the oven. A couple of recipes in this book call for cooking food on a rack on top of the sheet pan as well as inside it; some pans come with racks when you buy them, which is great but not essential. An ordinary metal rack, or even the oven rack itself, can serve the purpose by simply sitting on top.

A final word on the vagaries of ovens: for a variety of reasons, all ovens have their own temperaments. Age, make, model, insulation and settings are all factors that can affect the accuracy of an oven's temperature reading, and therefore the expected time it takes a dish to cook. What's more, heat can vary across different parts of the oven chamber, so even using an oven thermometer does not completely solve the problem. Sheet pan cooking is a brilliantly convenient way to cook, but you can't just wander off; it requires you to keep an occasional eye on things, turn the pan round now and then (except when baking cakes, as the sudden drop in temperature can cause your masterpiece to sink or crack) and keep your senses alert for when the dish is done.

Happy sheet pan cooking!

Breakfast
+
Brunch

Roast pear and rhubarb compote

Tongue-tingling rhubarb and sweet fragrant pears are always a heady combination, and the Christmassy notes from the spices mean there's a whole lot to love in a bowl of this compote. It also makes an easy dessert; swap the yogurt for some lightly whipped vanilla-spiked cream, and maybe some ginger cookies crumbled on top instead of nuts.

14oz rhubarb, cut into 2½-in pieces, sliced lengthways if very thick
4 ripe but firm Conference or Bartlett pears
squeeze of lemon juice
⅔ cup granulated sugar
1 cinnamon stick
2 cloves
1 star anise

To serve:
Greek yogurt
4 tbsp chopped toasted hazelnuts

Serves: 4 | Takes: 25 minutes

Preheat the oven to 400°F.

Place the rhubarb in a 8 x 12 x 2-in sheet pan. Peel, core and chop the pears into pieces the length and width of your index finger. Add them to the pan as you go, tossing with a little lemon juice to prevent discoloration.

Sprinkle the sugar over the fruit and add the spices to the pan. Toss to combine well, then cover tightly with foil and roast for 15 minutes. Remove the foil; the fruit should be very tender but if not, return to the oven, uncovered, for a further 5 minutes or so.

Serve the compote and the pan juices with a spoonful of yogurt and the hazelnuts sprinkled over the top.

Dutch pancake with raisins, orange blossom and marmalade

Making one big pancake is much easier than standing at the stove endlessly flipping, and this one is gorgeously fragrant with oranges and raisins. If you are not in possession of marmalade, or if you aren't partial to it, just use a good-quality jam or fruit compote of your choice.

2 tbsp vegetable oil
1 cup all-purpose flour
2 tbsp unrefined granulated sugar
pinch of salt
3 large eggs, lightly beaten
1¼ cups milk
2 tsp orange blossom water
1 tsp vanilla extract
finely grated zest of 1 orange
scant ½ cup mixed raisins
good-quality marmalade, to serve

Serves: 4 | Takes: 35 minutes

Preheat the oven to 425°F. Pour the vegetable oil into a 8 x 12 x 2-in sheet pan and place inside the oven to heat.

Whisk the flour, sugar and salt together in a mixing bowl. Whisk the eggs, milk, orange blossom water, vanilla and orange zest together in a jug. Gradually stir the wet ingredients into the dry, incorporating the flour as you go to make a smooth batter.

Working quickly, remove the sheet pan from the oven and pour in the batter. Sprinkle over the raisins and gently nudge them under the batter if necessary. Return to the oven and bake for 20 minutes, or until puffed, golden and just cooked through. Serve hot, spread with the marmalade.

Shakshuka

This version of the now famous North African dish is super easy as it completely cooks itself in the oven, allowing you to get on with important stuff like reading the weekend papers.

1 large red onion, halved and thickly
   sliced, layers separated
2 large red bell peppers, sliced
2 tbsp olive oil
7oz chorizo, cut into ¾-in cubes
2 x 14-oz cans chopped tomatoes
3 garlic cloves, crushed
2 tsp hot paprika
2 tsp ground cumin
1 heaped tbsp rose harissa paste
4–6 large eggs
1⅓ cups crumbled feta cheese
handful of cilantro leaves and tender
   stems, roughly chopped

Serves: 4–6 | Takes: 1 hour 10 minutes

Preheat the oven to 400°F.

Place all the ingredients, except the eggs, feta and cilantro, in a 8 x 12 x 2-in sheet pan. Add ⅔ cup water and stir well so all the ingredients are combined. Bake for 45 minutes, stirring frequently and adding a splash more water towards the end of cooking if needed to prevent the sauce becoming too thick.

Make indentations in the sauce with a spoon and crack in the eggs. Bake for about 10 minutes more, but watch the eggs carefully so the yolks don't overcook: the yolks need to be gooey. Sprinkle over the feta and cilantro and serve immediately.

Cinnamon French toast

French toast is really just an excuse to eat dessert for breakfast, but who's arguing? Baguette is specified here because it lends a little crunch and chewiness to proceedings, but slices of brioche or white bread also work well. Just make sure the slices are in a single layer in the sheet pan.

unsalted butter, for greasing
4 large eggs
generous ¾ cup milk
1½ tsp vanilla extract
1 tsp mixed spice
4 tbsp superfine sugar
12 slices of baguette, preferably stale,
    cut ⅝in thick on the diagonal
maple syrup, for drizzling

Serves: 4 | Takes: 25 minutes,
    plus 30 minutes soaking

Generously butter a 8 x 12 x 2-in sheet pan.

Whisk the eggs, milk, vanilla, mixed spice and sugar together in a shallow bowl.

Dip the bread slices into the egg mixture, giving both sides a really good soak. Transfer to the prepared sheet pan in a single layer—the slices should fit snugly. Pour over any remaining egg mixture and leave to soak for 30 minutes, turning over the bread slices halfway through. Meanwhile, preheat the oven to 400°F.

Bake for 15 minutes, or until the bread is puffed and golden. Serve hot, drizzled with maple syrup.

Berry and banana breakfast traybake

Oats, nuts, fruit and yogurt—sounds like breakfast, but tastes like afternoon tea, so what's not to like? There might be a lot of ingredients here but it's incredibly easy to pull together and results in an ultra-moist and flavorsome breakfast that's portable if you need it to be.

1⅓ cups all-purpose flour
1 cup rolled oats
⅓ cup unrefined superfine sugar
1 tsp baking powder
1 tsp baking soda
¼ tsp fine sea salt
1½ tsp ground cinnamon
⅓ cup raisins
¼ cup pecan nuts, roughly chopped
2 large ripe bananas
2 large eggs
generous ¾ cup Greek yogurt
1 tsp vanilla extract
finely grated zest of ½ lemon
5 tbsp mild olive oil
generous ¾ cup blueberries
1–2 tbsp dark brown soft sugar

Makes: 12 squares | Takes: 40 minutes

Preheat the oven to 350°F. Butter a 8 x 12 x 2-in sheet pan and line with baking parchment.

Whisk the flour, oats, sugar, baking powder, baking soda, salt and cinnamon together in a mixing bowl. Stir in the raisins and pecans.

Mash the bananas with a fork in a jug until sloppy, then add the remaining ingredients, except the blueberries and dark brown sugar, and mix well.

Stir the wet ingredients into the dry until just combined—some lumps and small bits of dry ingredients are fine. Pour into the prepared sheet pan and smooth the top with a spatula. Scatter the blueberries evenly over the top and push them gently into batter—you don't want them to disappear, just half buried. Sprinkle over the brown sugar.

Bake for 25 minutes, or until golden and an inserted skewer comes out clean. Cut into 12 squares and serve warm or cold.

Classic full English breakfast

There are no bells or whistles here, and deliberately so. Some mornings demand a simple hearty breakfast that requires next to no effort—and this is it. Make the tea, read a newspaper and let the oven do the cooking: just attend to the sheet pan now and then.

olive oil, for brushing
4 good-quality sausages of your choice
8 cremini mushrooms
sea salt and freshly ground black pepper
4 smoked lean bacon slices
8 cherry tomatoes
2 slices of sourdough bread
2 large eggs

Serves: 2 | Takes: about 35 minutes

Preheat the oven to 475°F. Lightly brush a 8 x 12 x 2-in sheet pan with olive oil and place in the oven to heat.

Place the sausages and mushrooms in the hot pan, and shake to lightly coat in the hot oil. Season with salt and pepper and roast for 6 minutes, shaking the pan about halfway through.

Reduce the oven temperature to 400°F. Add the bacon, tomatoes and bread slices, then season with more salt and pepper and shake the pan again. Roast for 20 minutes, shaking the pan and turning the bread over halfway through.

Make 2 spaces in the middle of the ingredients and crack in the eggs. Return to the oven for 6–8 minutes, or until the eggs are done to your liking. Serve immediately.

Potato, chorizo and mushroom hash with chili mayo

Hearty, spicy and warming, this is a restorative breakfast of the highest order. If you feel inclined, throw in some finely sliced greens like chard or spinach when you return the chorizo to the pan for the final 5 minutes.

8½oz chorizo sausage (not cooking chorizo)
splash of olive oil
1¼lb potatoes, unpeeled, cut into ¾-in cubes
sea salt and freshly ground black pepper
5oz cremini mushrooms, finely sliced

For the chili mayo:
⅓ cup good-quality mayonnaise
1 tbsp chipotle paste or other chili paste, or more to taste
squeeze of lime juice
splash of olive oil, to loosen

Serves: 2 generously | Takes: 50 minutes

Preheat the oven to 400°F. Cut the chorizo into ½-in coins, then cut each coin in half. Place in a 8 x 12 x 2-in sheet pan, drizzle over a little olive oil and roast for 10 minutes until it starts to crisp at the edges and release its spicy oil.

Scoop the chorizo out of the pan with a slotted spoon and transfer to a bowl, leaving the spicy oil in the pan. Add the potatoes to the pan, season with salt and pepper and toss well to coat. Roast for 20 minutes, shaking the pan occasionally.

Add the mushrooms to the sheet pan, toss in the oil and roast for a further 10 minutes. Return the chorizo to the pan and roast for a final 5 minutes.

Meanwhile, stir all the ingredients for the chili mayonnaise together in a bowl to combine.

Serve the hash hot with the chili mayonnaise spooned over.

Baked apple oatmeal with chia seeds, raisins and macadamia nuts

Why stand at the stove stirring an oatmeal pot when you can toss the ingredients in a sheet pan and go back to bed for 30 minutes while it cooks? This is oatmeal as it should be: creamy and brimming with the flavor of apples, cinnamon and nuts.

unsalted butter, for greasing
2 cups rolled oats
2 tbsp chia seeds
2 eating apples, peeled, cored and chopped into small cubes
½ cup raisins
½ cup macadamia nuts or blanched hazelnuts, roughly chopped
2 tsp ground cinnamon
½ tsp fine sea salt
1¼ cups milk
3 tbsp honey
light brown soft sugar, for sprinkling

To serve (optional):
yogurt or milk
fresh fruit of choice

Serves: 6 | Takes: 40 minutes

Preheat the oven to 325°F. Lightly butter a 8 x 12 x 2-in sheet pan.

Stir the oatmeal, chia seeds, apples, raisins, nuts, cinnamon and salt together in a large bowl. Stir in 1½ cups boiling water, the milk and honey. Pour the mixture into the prepared pan and bake for 30 minutes.

Remove the pan from the oven and stir the oatmeal thoroughly, adding a splash more water if needed to produce the desired thickness. Sprinkle over the sugar and bake for a further 5 minutes. Serve hot with yogurt or milk and some fresh fruit, if you like.

Oat and buckwheat granola

The buckwheat flakes give this a slightly nutty, somehow more grown-up flavor than granola made solely with oats as the base—but it's not too overpowering.

1½ cups rolled oats
1 cup buckwheat flakes
scant ¾ cup mixed nuts, such as almonds, pistachios, pecans and macadamia nuts, roughly chopped
scant ¼ cup mixed seeds
¼ tsp fine sea salt
1 tsp ground cinnamon
1 tbsp vegetable oil
4 tbsp maple syrup
1 tbsp honey
1 tsp vanilla extract
½ cup mixed dried fruit of choice, chopped
scant ¼ cup dry unsweetened coconut

Makes: 15oz | Serves 4–6
Takes: 1 hour 15 minutes

Preheat the oven to 300°F and line a 8 x 12 x 2-in sheet pan with baking parchment. Add the oats, buckwheat flakes, nuts, seeds, salt and cinnamon to the pan and stir well to combine.

Mix the vegetable oil, maple syrup, honey and vanilla together in a jug, then pour over the oat mixture. Stir until the dry ingredients are coated—you might think there's not enough liquid but keep mixing until everything looks slightly damp.

Spread the mixture out in the pan and bake for 50 minutes, until lightly golden, shaking the pan regularly. The granola will crisp up as it cools.

Transfer the mixture to a large bowl, add the dried fruit and coconut and mix until evenly distributed. Allow to cool before storing in an airtight container for up to 1 month.

Baked ruby grapefruit with spices and brown sugar

Broiled grapefruit is a breakfast classic, but this recipe rings some changes. Baking instead of broiling softens the whole fruit rather than just the top, coaxing out the juices and mellowing the delicious tartness. Cutting the grapefruit into segments before cooking allows the sugar to seep right through and makes eating it easier, of course.

1 ruby grapefruit
2 generous pinches of ground cinnamon
2 generous pinches of ground ginger
2 heaped tsp raw brown sugar
Greek yogurt, to serve

Serves: 2 | Takes: 15 minutes

Preheat the oven to 425°F. Cut the grapefruit in half across the equator. Cut between the flesh and the white pith of each half with a small, serrated knife, working at an angle to reach the bottom of the fruit. Slice along the membranes.

Place the grapefruit halves, cut-side up, in a 8 x 12 x 2-in sheet pan and sprinkle over the cinnamon, ginger, then the sugar.

Bake for 10 minutes until the sugar has melted. Serve immediately with Greek yogurt.

Quick croque madame

A truly authentic croque boasts a layer of creamy béchamel sauce, but this is equally tasty—and saves you a good amount of cooking and washing up. It makes a perfect breakfast or brunch—just scale up the recipe according to the number of mouths to feed. A 8 x 12 x 2-in sheet pan should fit 4–6 croques.

olive oil, for brushing
salted butter, for buttering
1 large slice of sourdough or country-
    style bread
good-quality mayonnaise or Dijon
    mustard or both, for spreading
1 large thick slice of ham
1 large egg
⅓ cup grated Gruyère cheese

Makes: 1 | Takes: 20 minutes

Preheat the oven to 400°F and lightly brush a 8 x 12 x 2-in sheet pan with olive oil.

Generously butter both sides of the bread. Stamp a circle out of the center of the bread using a cutter or eggcup a little larger than an egg yolk. Spread the top of the bread with mayonnaise and/or mustard.

Place the bread and the stamped out circle in the pan. Top the bread with the ham—you will have to cut it so it doesn't cover the hole.

Carefully crack the egg into the hole so that it holds the yolk. Scatter the cheese over the top so that the bread, ham and egg are covered.

Bake for 12–15 minutes, or until the cheese has melted, the egg white is set and the yolk is still a little gooey. Serve immediately.

Cheese and bacon swirls

Rolling out of bed and straight into a baking session might not sound appealing, but honestly this is so easy. The tiny effort involved in wrapping pastry around bacon and cheese will be amply rewarded, and beats an early-morning trip to the shops for pastries.

1 sheet ready-rolled puff pastry,
    or 11¼oz block pastry
all-purpose flour, for dusting
1⅓ cups grated cheddar cheese
4¼oz bacon, chopped into small pieces
1 scallion, finely chopped
1 large egg, lightly beaten

Makes: 12 | Takes: 40 minutes,
    plus 20 minutes chilling

Preheat the oven to 350°F and line a 8 x 12 x 2-in sheet pan with baking parchment.

Lay the pastry sheet on a lightly floured work surface or, if using a block, roll out into a 10 x 12-in rectangle. Scatter over the cheese, bacon and scallion. Roll the pastry from the short end into a tight log and chill in the fridge for 20 minutes.

Cut the log into 12 equal slices and arrange them cut-side up and spaced apart in the prepared sheet pan. Press them down to flatten a little, then brush the tops with beaten egg.

Bake for 25–30 minutes, or until puffed and golden. Serve warm.

Snacks
+
Light Bites

Parmesan, garlic and poppy seed crackers

These delicious salty bites go perfectly with drinks—much nicer than a bowl of chips. Don't be tempted to cook them for longer than suggested, as not much stands between perfectly cooked and burnt. A tip for garlic granules that (inevitably, it seems) clump together: pop a chunk in a mortar and pound with a pestle to make a powder.

generous ¾ cup finely grated Parmesan cheese
½ tsp poppy seeds
¼ tsp garlic granules

Makes: about 12 | Takes: 15 minutes

Preheat the oven to 350°F and line a 8 x 12 x 2-in sheet pan with baking parchment.

Mix all the ingredients together in a bowl. Place 1 level tbsp of the mixture in the prepared pan in equally spaced mounds. Flatten with the back of a spoon to make disks, about 2½in wide. Bake for 7 minutes, or until just turning pale gold at the edges.

Leave in the pan for 2 minutes, then transfer to paper towels with a spatula to cool and crisp up. Store in an airtight container for up to 2 days.

Baked figs, halloumi, prosciutto and basil

It's quite easy for one person to put away a whole batch of these; the combination of salty ham and melted cheese with the sweet figs is heavenly, especially served hot from the oven. Serve them as a lovely appetizer with a few bitter salad greens, or a decadent bite with drinks.

olive oil, for greasing and drizzling
6½oz halloumi cheese
12 large basil leaves
6 large ripe figs, halved lengthwise
12 long slices of prosciutto ham, about 3½oz
1 tbsp honey, or to taste (optional)

Makes: 12 | Takes: 15 minutes

Preheat the oven to 400°F and lightly oil a 8 x 12 x 2-in sheet pan.

Cut the halloumi into six ¼-in slices, then cut each slice in half to make 12 small rectangles.

Fold a basil leaf in half, place it on the cut side of a fig half and top with a piece of halloumi. Wrap in a piece of prosciutto and transfer to the sheet pan. Repeat.

Drizzle with olive oil and roast for 10 minutes, or until the prosciutto is starting to crisp up and the halloumi is hot. Serve immediately, drizzled with honey, if you like.

Massively cheesy cheese and garlic pull-apart rolls

Pulling these rolls apart is one thing; tearing yourself away from the vicinity of the pan is a trickier task entirely. Loads of cheese, garlic and bread together in a group hug—there's nothing more to say.

8 tbsp unsalted butter, softened
4 garlic cloves, crushed
3½ cups strong white bread flour, plus extra for dusting
1 tbsp granulated sugar
1 tsp sea salt
¾oz fast-action dried yeast
1¼ cups milk
8½oz fresh mozzarella cheese, cut into 12 equal chunks, plus an extra 4½oz, chopped
1 large egg, lightly beaten
1½ cups grated sharp cheddar cheese

Makes: 12 | Takes: 40 minutes, plus 20 minutes resting

Preheat the oven to 400°F. Mix the butter and garlic together in a small bowl. Transfer the butter to a 8 x 12 x 2-in sheet pan and place inside the oven for a few minutes to melt—don't let the garlic color.

Combine the flour, sugar, salt and yeast together in a large mixing bowl. Make a well in the center and pour in the milk and warm garlic butter from the sheet pan. Make sure you scrape all the garlic into the bowl. Mix until everything comes together into a rough dough. Set aside for 10 minutes covered with a clean cloth. Meanwhile, brush the residual butter left in the pan up the sides.

Knead the dough on a lightly floured work surface for 10 minutes, or for 8 minutes in an electric mixer with a dough hook attachment. It should be soft and elastic and come away easily from the work surface or the sides of the bowl. Divide into 12 pieces, roughly 2¾oz each, and roll into balls.

Press a ball into a 4-in disk on a lightly floured surface. Place a mozzarella chunk in the center, bring the dough up over the cheese and pinch the edges together to seal tightly. Turn over and shape into a ball. Repeat with the rest of dough and mozzarella. Arrange the balls in the sheet pan to make three rows of four equally spaced apart. Cover with a clean cloth and leave for 10 minutes.

Brush the tops of the rolls with the beaten egg, then tuck the remaining mozzarella and the cheddar cheese into the gaps. Bake for 20 minutes until risen and golden.

Ricotta, asparagus and mint tartlets

The lemon and mint makes these tartlets sing: they're a perfect springtime lunch or appetizer when tender asparagus is in season and at its very best. Serve with a good mixed salad.

⅓ cup ricotta cheese
2 heaped tbsp finely grated
    Parmesan cheese
1 large egg, beaten
grated zest of ½ lemon
½ tbsp olive oil, plus extra for drizzling
1 tbsp chopped mint, plus extra for
    sprinkling
sea salt and freshly ground black pepper
1 x 10½-oz sheet of ready-rolled puff
    pastry or 11¼oz block pastry (keep
    chilled until needed)
24 fine asparagus spears, trimmed to
    about 5in

Makes: 4 | Takes: 35 minutes

Preheat the oven to 350°F and line a 8 x 12 x 2-in sheet pan with baking parchment.

Beat the ricotta, Parmesan, 2 tablespoons of the beaten egg, the lemon zest, olive oil, mint and salt and pepper together in a bowl.

Trim the pastry sheet, or roll out the block, into a 12 x 8-in rectangle. Cut in half crossways and lengthways to make four 6 x 4-in rectangles, and transfer to the prepared sheet pan.

Mark a ½-in border around each pastry rectangle with the tines of a fork and brush the border with the remaining beaten egg. Prick inside the border with the fork. Divide the ricotta mixture between each tartlet and spread out inside the border. Top with the asparagus spears, drizzle with a little olive oil and sprinkle over more mint and salt. Bake for 25 minutes, or until puffed and golden.

Serve immediately.

Roast buttered almonds with honey and chile

These are super tasty, take virtually no effort at all and make a lovely snack. An added bonus is that your kitchen will be filled with the wonderful smell of toasted nuts and butter.

3 tbsp unsalted butter
3 tbsp honey
1 tsp red pepper flakes
1½ cups blanched almonds
sea salt flakes

Makes: a small bowlful
Takes: about 25 minutes

Preheat the oven to 325°F. Place the butter in a 8 x 12 x 2-in sheet pan and transfer to the oven for 2 minutes to melt.

Remove the pan from the oven and stir the honey and red pepper flakes into the melted butter. Add the almonds and toss to coat, ensuring they are spread out in a single layer.

Roast for 20–25 minutes, or until the nuts are golden—keep an eye on them, as they burn easily, and shake the pan occasionally. Sprinkle with salt. Delicious served warm—the nuts will crisp up as they cool a little.

Tuna, caper and onion mini pies

Blink and they're gone: that's what happens when you make these gorgeous mini pies. There's something about the combination of flavors that make them completely addictive, especially eaten hot, straight out of the oven.

7oz canned tuna in oil (drained weight)
scant ½ cup finely chopped onion
2 tbsp capers, rinsed, drained and
    finely chopped
½ red bell pepper, seeded and
    finely chopped
7 tbsp cream cheese
1 tsp smoked paprika
sea salt and freshly ground black pepper
2 sheets of ready-rolled shortcrust pastry,
    about 11¼oz each
1 egg, lightly beaten

Makes: 12 | Takes: 45 minutes

Preheat the oven to 400°F and line a 8 x 12 x 2-in sheet pan with baking parchment.

Mix all the ingredients, except the pastry and egg, together in a bowl until completely combined. The cream cheese should bind everything together.

Using a plate or bowl as guide, cut twelve 2½-in circles from the pastry sheets. Lightly brush the edges with a little of the beaten egg. Place equal quantities of the tuna mixture along the center of each circle—a dessertspoonful is about right. Pick a circle up with your hands, fold it in half and gently press the edges together, then pleat, to seal. Repeat with the remaining pastry and filling, transferring to the sheet pan as you go. Brush the tops with the remaining beaten egg.

Bake for 30–35 minutes until beautifully golden. Eat the pies as soon as they are cool enough to do so safely.

(Pictured overleaf)

Sweet potato and corn fritters

These are deeeelicious. You could eat them as a side or appetizer, maybe with a bowl of guacamole alongside, or gobble them hot straight from the sheet pan with a squeeze of lime and a sprinkling of good sea salt flakes.

7oz sweet potatoes, grated
¾ cup corn kernels (fresh or from a can)
1 tbsp self-rising flour
1 fat garlic clove, crushed
generous ¼ cup finely grated Parmesan cheese
1 large egg
2 tsp Aleppo pepper (or 2 tsp sweet paprika plus a generous pinch of cayenne)
½ tsp sea salt

Makes: 8 | Takes: 35 minutes

Preheat the oven to 400°F and line a 8 x 12 x 2-in sheet pan with baking parchment.

Place all the ingredients in a bowl and mix well. Drop 8 equal mounds of the mixture into the prepared sheet pan and flatten them slightly with a fork.

Roast for 25 minutes, or until they are starting to crisp up at the edges and can be easily flipped with a spatula. Turn over and roast for a further 5 minutes. Serve immediately.

Potato rösti with smoked ham and eggs

Just a handful of humble ingredients come together here for a joyous lunch (or even breakfast) that's far easier to make in a sheet pan than in a frying pan. As ever, keep your eyes glued to the eggs as they bake: all ovens are different and you want the yolks to spill their loveliness over the rösti when you cut into them, not require a carving knife.

3 tbsp duck or goose fat, or olive oil
4 medium waxy potatoes,
    about 6½oz each
4 thick slices of smoked ham,
    about 1½oz each, chopped
sea salt flakes and freshly ground
    black pepper
4 large eggs

Makes: 4 | Takes: about 45 minutes

Preheat the oven to 400°F. Place the fat or olive oil in a 8 x 12 x 2-in sheet pan to melt and/or get hot.

Grate the potatoes into a bowl—you can peel them if you like, but the skin adds flavor. Add the ham, season with salt and pepper and mix well.

Spoon 4 mounds of potato into the prepared sheet pan, and gently spread into circles, about ⅝in high. Spoon a little of the hot fat or oil over the top of each one. Roast for 30 minutes, or until golden at the edges and beginning to turn brown on top.

Make an indentation in each rösti with the back of a soup spoon and crack in an egg. Return to the oven for a further 6–8 minutes, or until the whites are just set and the yolks are still runny. Serve immediately.

Grilled cheese with apple, thyme and mustard

There's nothing wrong with simple grilled cheese, of course, but the addition of apple or pear and fragrant herbs elevates this iconic snack to something gorgeous. It's lovely to have a mix of cheese: Comté or Gruyère for gooeyness and sharp cheddar for punchy flavor.

oil, for greasing
salted butter, for spreading
2 slices of bloomer or other white bread
Dijon or seedy mustard, for spreading
scant ¼ cup grated Gruyère cheese,
    Comté or mozzarella cheese
¼ cup grated sharp cheddar or other
    flavorsome cheese
½ apple or pear, finely sliced
about ¼ tsp chopped thyme leaves

Serves: 1 (but can easily be scaled up
    to make 2–3 in the same pan)
Takes: 15 minutes

Preheat the oven to 425°F and lightly oil a 8 x 12 x 2-in sheet pan. Place it in the oven to heat.

Butter the bread on both sides, then spread mustard on one slice. Top the mustardy slice with the cheeses, apple or pear and thyme. Place the other bread slice on top and press together.

Place the sandwich in the hot sheet pan and place a baking sheet or ovenproof pan on top—this will press the sandwich together like a panini. Bake for 10 minutes, or until the top and the bottom of the sandwich are golden and the cheese melted. Serve immediately.

Tortilla chips with garlic and chipotle salt

This is unashamedly a cheat's version of those addictive bagged snacks that turn your fingers fluorescent orange. These tortillas are fresher, tastier and healthier, as they're not deep-fried. The golden rule is to watch the chips like a hawk, as they burn in a flash.

1 good-quality corn tortilla per batch
1 tsp garlic-flavored olive oil, or plain is fine
sea salt flakes
chipotle powder or smoked paprika
garlic granules

Makes: 8 chips per batch
Takes: 10 minutes per batch

Preheat the oven to 350°F.

Lightly brush the tortilla on both sides with oil, making sure you brush right up to the edges. Using a pizza cutter or sharp knife, cut into 8 equal pieces. Arrange in a single layer in a 8 x 12 x 2-in sheet pan and bake for 5–6 minutes, turning over halfway through. They will crisp up more as they cool.

While the chips are hot, sprinkle with salt, chipotle powder or paprika and garlic granules.

Lamb, pistachio and mint sausage rolls

Who doesn't love a sausage roll? Spiced meat encased in buttery puff pastry, eaten warm and dunked in ketchup, with a cold drink on the side, is one of life's absolute pleasures.

2¼ cups ground lamb
½ onion, grated
scant ¼ cup chopped pistachio nuts
1 tbsp chipotle paste
½ cup chopped mint leaves
2 garlic cloves, crushed
sea salt and freshly ground black pepper
1 x 11¾-oz sheet of ready-rolled puff
  pastry or 11¾oz block pastry
all-purpose flour, for dusting
1 large egg, lightly beaten

Makes: 12 small sausage rolls
Takes: 50 minutes

Preheat the oven to 425°F and line a 8 x 12 x 2-in sheet pan with baking parchment.

Place the lamb, onion, pistachios, chipotle paste, mint and garlic in a bowl. Season generously with salt and pepper and mix well with your hands until everything is combined.

Roll out the pastry sheet or block on a lightly floured work surface into a square roughly 14 x 14in. Fold the pastry in half, lightly press to make a crease, then unfold and cut along the line to make 2 rectangles, 14 x 7in.

Place half the meat mixture down the center of one of the rectangles of pastry in a sausage shape. Brush the edges of the pastry with a little of the beaten egg, then firmly roll it up and seal well. Repeat with the remaining lamb mixture and pastry rectangle. Seal the rolls well.

Trim the ends, then cut each pastry log into 6 equal pieces. Make a couple of slits in the top of each piece and transfer to the prepared sheet pan.

Brush the tops of the sausage rolls with the remaining beaten egg and bake for 25 minutes until puffed and golden. Serve warm.

Crispy chicken scratchings

These are a bit naughty: chicken skin bites baked to salty crispness. Ask your butcher for the skins, or remove them from chicken breasts, drumsticks and thighs.

8¾oz chicken skin
sea salt flakes

Makes: 1 bowlful | Takes: 30 minutes

Preheat the oven to 350°F.

Cut the chicken skin into pieces, roughly 1½-in square—the exact size doesn't matter, so long as they're equal and not too small. Place in a single layer in a 8 x 12 x 2-in sheet pan and sprinkle with salt.

Bake for about 30 minutes, shaking the pan every 10 minutes and pouring out the rendered fat each time (save it to use instead of oil or duck fat in another dish).

Tip the scratchings onto paper towels, sprinkle with a little more salt if needed, and serve immediately.

Pizza bianca

This is such glorious pizza: garlicky, chewy and simple. Adorn with anything you fancy—curls of wafer-thin prosciutto and cheese are delicious. Or serve with a bowl of good extra virgin olive oil on the side for dunking, and a bowl of olives.

3½ cups strong white bread flour, plus extra for dusting (optional)
1½ tsp fast-action dried yeast
1½ tsp sea salt
2 tbsp olive oil, plus extra for oiling and drizzling
cornstarch, for dusting
sea salt flakes
2 large rosemary sprigs, leaves removed and chopped

Makes: 2 pizzas | Takes: 40 minutes, plus 3 hours rising

Using an electric mixer or a mixing bowl, whisk the flour, yeast and salt together. Stir in 1½ cups warm water and the olive oil. Use a dough hook to knead for 5–8 minutes, or turn onto a lightly floured surface and knead by hand for 10 minutes, until smooth and elastic. Place in an oiled bowl, cover with plastic wrap and leave to rise in a warm place for 2 hours.

Punch down the dough, divide into 2 equal pieces and roll into sausages. Lightly flour the work surface with cornstarch and leave the dough to rest on it covered with a clean cloth for 1 hour. After 30 minutes, preheat the oven to its highest setting and place a 8 x 12 x 2-in sheet pan inside to heat.

Cut out a piece of baking parchment, 8 x 12in, and place a piece of dough in the middle. Stretch and press the dough out with your fingertips to cover the paper—it should be nice and dimpled. Carefully transfer the dough and paper to the hot sheet pan, sprinkle generously with salt and half the rosemary and drizzle with olive oil.

Bake for 12–15 minutes until the crust is golden with a few dark spots. Serve hot from the oven and repeat with the remaining dough.

(Pictured overleaf)

Garlicky mushroom and thyme tartines

Tartine is a fancy name for loaded toast, and this one makes an excellent light lunch. A mixture of mushrooms, including wild ones, would be perfect, but large Portobellos or flat caps on their own work nicely.

extra virgin olive oil, for brushing
  and drizzling
4¼oz mixed mushrooms
3½ tbsp unsalted butter, softened
generous ¼ cup grated Parmesan cheese
1 garlic clove, crushed
1 heaped tsp finely chopped thyme
finely grated zest of ½ lemon
sea salt and freshly ground black pepper
2 large slices of sourdough or good-
  quality country-style bread

Makes: 2 large tartines
Takes: 25 minutes

Preheat the oven to 425°F and brush a 8 x 12 x 2-in sheet pan with olive oil.

Finely chop half the mushrooms and place in a medium bowl. Add the butter, Parmesan, garlic, thyme, lemon zest and salt and pepper. Mix until well combined and roughly spreadable.

Spread equal amounts of the mixture over the bread slices and transfer to the sheet pan.

Slice the remaining mushrooms into bite-size pieces and arrange on top of the mushroom mixture. Drizzle with olive oil and season with salt and pepper.

Roast for 15 minutes, or until the mushrooms are tender and the bottom of the bread is crisp and golden. Serve hot.

Lunch
+
Warm Salads

Spinach, bacon and double cheese bake

Something magical happens when eggs, cream, cheese, smoky bacon and vegetables are united. This dish is lovely served with a crisp green salad and also wonderful popped in lunchboxes the next day, if there's any left over.

3 medium waxy potatoes, about 14oz, peeled and cut into ¾-in cubes
1 red onion, quartered, layers separated
1 tbsp extra virgin olive oil
sea salt and freshly ground black pepper
5¼oz smoked bacon lardons
8 large eggs, lightly beaten
1 cup heavy cream
¾ cup grated Parmesan cheese
1 cup grated mozzarella cheese
1 cup spinach leaves, finely sliced
2 garlic cloves, crushed
1 tsp sea salt flakes

Serves: 6 | Takes: 1 hour

Preheat the oven to 400°F.

Place the potatoes and onion in a 8 x 12 x 2-in sheet pan, toss with the olive oil and season with salt and pepper. Roast for 15 minutes, shaking the pan occasionally. Add the lardons to the pan, shake well and roast for a further 10 minutes.

Meanwhile, stir the eggs and cream together in a large bowl. Stir in the cheeses, spinach, garlic, the 1 teaspoon of sea salt flakes and some pepper and mix well.

When the vegetables and lardons have done their time in the oven, loosen them with a spatula to ensure they're not sticking to the bottom of the pan. Pour in the egg mixture and use a wooden spoon to nudge the vegetables around so they're evenly distributed and the spinach is almost submerged in the liquid. Bake for 20–25 minutes, or until puffed and golden and the eggs are just set. Let the pan stand for 5 minutes before cutting into squares to serve.

Baked whole camembert with rosemary, honey and garlic toast

This is so lovely and decadent, with the warm gooey interior perfect for dunking with crunchy, garlicky spears of toast. It's very easy to eat a whole one yourself, but share if you have to.

2 garlic cloves
4 slices of sourdough bread or similar
extra virgin olive oil, for drizzling
1 whole Camembert, about 8¾oz
1 tsp honey, plus extra to serve
8 rosemary tips

Optional extras for dunking:
pickles
Parma ham
sliced fruit, such as figs, pears or apples

Serves: 1–2 | Takes: 20 minutes

Preheat the oven to 400°F.

Cut one of the garlic cloves in half and rub on both sides of the bread with the cut side. Drizzle both sides with olive oil and place in a 8 x 12 x 2-in sheet pan.

Take the cheese out of its box, remove the paper wrapping and return it to the box. (If the cheese doesn't come in a box, place in a small baking pot.) Cut four long deep slashes in the cheese, and spoon in the honey.

Cut the remaining garlic into slivers, including what's left of the clove used to rub the bread, and poke into the slashes. Poke the rosemary tips in, too. Drizzle with olive oil and place in the sheet pan alongside the bread.

Bake for 15 minutes until the cheese is bubbling and the bread toasted and golden. Serve immediately with any optional extras for dunking.

Spicy cheese and bacon burgers

It's fair to say these don't have the charred exterior of burgers cooked on the grill—but what they can boast is a tender, juicy interior that's absolutely packed with flavor. No dried-out burgers in this sheet pan.

olive oil, for brushing
2¼ cups ground beef, ideally 20% fat
2 smoked bacon slices, finely chopped
1 tbsp sriracha sauce (if you have none, or don't like spice, tomato ketchup is fine)
sea salt flakes and freshly ground black pepper
1 large onion, finely sliced
4 Monterey Jack or Gouda cheese slices
4 burger buns, toasted if you like
sliced tomatoes and lettuce, to serve

Serves: 4 | Takes: 30 minutes

Preheat the oven to 350°F and brush a 8 x 12 x 2-in sheet pan with olive oil.

Place the beef, bacon, sriracha and salt and pepper in a bowl and mix with your hands until everything is well combined. Shape the mixture into four equal-sized patties, about ⅝in high—don't pack them too tightly, just enough to keep their shape.

Spread the onion out in the pan and place the burgers on top. Roast for about 15 minutes, flipping halfway through. Top each burger with a cheese slice and roast for a further 5 minutes. The burger should feel slightly springy to touch.

Serve the burgers and onions stuffed between the buns with some tomato and lettuce.

Chicken fajitas

There's something universally appealing about a self-assembly meal. This version is the simplest of all—a whack-it-all-in-the-pan affair that barely constitutes cooking. And it's really tasty.

For the chicken:
3 boneless and skinless chicken
    breasts, cut into thin strips
1 large red bell pepper, cut into
    thin strips
1 tbsp smoked paprika
1 tsp ground cumin
2 tsp dried oregano
1 tsp cayenne pepper or chili powder
juice of 1 lime
2 tbsp olive oil

For the salsa:
1 bunch of cilantro
1 fat garlic clove, crushed
2 large ripe tomatoes
juice of ½ lime, plus extra to taste
3 tbsp extra virgin olive oil

corn tortilla wraps, to serve

Optional toppings including:
grated cheddar cheese, guacamole,
    shredded lettuce, crème fraîche

Serves: 4 | Takes: 35 minutes

Preheat the oven to 400°F and place a 8 x 12 x 2-in sheet pan or oven dish inside to heat.

Place all the chicken ingredients in a bowl and toss with your hands until everything is coated in a slick of spiced oil. Set aside for 5 minutes.

Meanwhile, roughly chop the cilantro leaves and tender stems and place in a bowl with the remaining salsa ingredients. Set aside.

Tip the chicken into the hot sheet pan. Roast for 20–25 minutes, shaking the pan occasionally, until the chicken is cooked through.

Serve wrapped in tortillas with the tomato salsa and your choice of toppings.

Fish and chips

The precise cooking time for the fish will depend on its thickness, but choose reasonably chunky fillets, or the crumb coating won't have time to crisp up and turn golden.

14oz large floury potatoes, such as Yukon Gold, Desirée or Russets
1 tbsp rapeseed oil, plus extra for drizzling
celery salt, herb salt or plain sea salt
2 cod, hake, plaice or other white fish fillets, about 4¼oz each, cut into 1½-in strips
⅓ cup all-purpose flour
1 large egg, lightly beaten
1 cup panko breadcrumbs
⅓ cup golden breadcrumbs
½ tsp smoked paprika
fine sea salt and freshly ground black pepper

Serves: 2 | Takes: 45 minutes

Preheat the oven to its maximum temperature. Place a 8 x 12 x 2-in sheet pan inside to heat. Have ready a wire rack that sits in or over the sheet pan.

Cut the potatoes into fries (chips) about ½in thick (peel them if you like, but the skin adds flavor). Transfer to a bowl of cold water as you go. Drain well and pat dry with paper towels. Return to the bowl, add the oil and salt and toss to coat. Carefully arrange in a single layer in the hot sheet pan. Roast for 15 minutes, shaking the pan occasionally.

Meanwhile, place the flour, egg and breadcrumbs in three separate shallow bowls. Stir the paprika into the flour and generously season with salt and pepper. Dredge the fish strips in the flour, then the egg and finally the breadcrumbs, pressing the breadcrumbs to encourage them to stick. Transfer to the wire rack and drizzle with oil.

When the fries have done their 15 minutes, flip them over with a spatula and reduce the oven temperature to 425°F. Sit the fish on its rack in or on the sheet pan and roast for about 20 minutes, or until the fish is cooked through and breadcrumbs are pale golden. Serve.

Warm salad of roast tomatoes, figs and feta with tarragon

You could replace half the tomatoes with a handful of mixed cherry tomatoes to add extra color and variety to this lovely salad.

6 medium tomatoes
6 fresh figs, stalks trimmed off
    and halved
8¾oz feta cheese, broken into
    large chunks
8¾oz sourdough bread, torn into chunks
3 tarragon stalks, leaves removed
extra virgin olive oil, for drizzling
sea salt flakes and freshly ground
    black pepper
squeeze of lemon, to serve

Serves: 4–6 | Takes: 30 minutes

Preheat the oven to 350°F.

Cut half the tomatoes in half and the remainder into quarters, and place in a 8 x 12 x 2-in sheet pan. Add the figs, feta, bread and tarragon, drizzle generously with olive oil and season with salt and pepper. Gently tumble everything together.

Roast for 25 minutes, shaking the pan occasionally, until the tomatoes and figs have collapsed down a little and released some of their juices, and the feta is golden at the edges.

Serve warm with a squeeze of lemon and more salt and pepper if needed.

Maple and lime-roasted squash with lentils, ricotta and basil oil

Fragrant and filling, this makes a sublime meat-free feast on a crisp fall day. The sweet comforting flavors of the mushrooms and squash work beautifully with the sprightly herb oil.

1lb 10oz peeled and seeded butternut squash, cut into 1¼-in chunks
3 tbsp olive oil, plus extra if needed and for drizzling
1 tbsp maple syrup
sea salt and freshly ground black pepper
2 bay leaves
1¼ cups cooked green lentils (canned lentils work well)
¾ tsp red pepper flakes
finely grated zest of 1 lime
3⅓ cups mixed mushrooms, such as Portobello or cremini, cut into thick slices
1 whole ricotta, about 8¾oz

For the basil oil:
1 cup basil leaves and fine stalks
3 tbsp lime juice (from the lime used for the zest)
2 garlic cloves
½ cup extra virgin olive oil

Serves: 4 | Takes: 1 hour

Preheat the oven to 425°F.

Place the squash in a 8 x 12 x 2-in sheet pan, drizzle with half the olive oil and all the maple syrup. Season with salt and pepper and toss to coat. Tuck the bay leaves into the pan and roast for 15 minutes.

While the squash is roasting, place the lentils in a small bowl and stir in the remaining olive oil, the red pepper flakes, lime zest and salt and pepper. Add to the pan with the squash, then add the mushrooms. Toss to combine, ensuring everything is lightly slicked with oil—add a little more oil if necessary.

Make space in the middle of the pan, add the ricotta and drizzle with oil. Roast for 35–40 minutes, or until the top of the ricotta is golden. Stir the lentils, squash and mushrooms occasionally to prevent them sticking and drying out.

Meanwhile, make the basil oil by blitzing all the ingredients in a food processor or pounding in a mortar with a pestle.

To serve, divide the ricotta, vegetables and lentils among serving plates and generously drizzle with the basil oil.

Warm salad of red cabbage, grapes and halloumi

This is an unusual but tasty winter salad—the cooked grapes provide a pop of sweetness that works beautifully with the salty cheese and earthy cabbage.

⅔ cup black seedless grapes,
    halved if large
2⅔ cups finely sliced red cabbage
3½oz halloumi cheese, cut into
    small cubes
¾oz pumpkin seeds
2 tbsp balsamic vinegar
5 tbsp olive oil
sea salt and freshly ground black pepper
1½ tbsp lime juice, plus extra to taste
½ tsp honey
generous pinch of red pepper flakes
handful of arugula, about ¾oz
⅛ cup flat leaf parsley, roughly chopped
⅛ cup cilantro, roughly chopped

Serves: 2–4 | Takes: 30 minutes

Preheat the oven to 400°F.

Place the grapes, cabbage, halloumi and pumpkin seeds in a 8 x 12 x 2-in sheet pan. Pour over the balsamic vinegar and 2 tablespoons of the olive oil, then season with salt and pepper and toss until everything is coated. Roast for 20 minutes or so until the grapes and cabbage are tender.

Meanwhile, whisk the remaining olive oil, the lime juice, honey, red pepper flakes and salt and pepper together to make a dressing.

Tip the contents of the sheet pan onto a serving platter. Add the arugula and herbs, and toss with the dressing, adding extra lime juice to taste. Serve immediately.

Creamy baked leeks with apple, thyme and goat cheese

Leeks, apple, cheese and cream parked in the same sheet pan is a very good thing indeed. This makes a fantastic meal served with a crunchy green salad dressed with a sharp vinaigrette.

1 tbsp unsalted butter, plus extra
   for greasing
18oz leeks, trimmed, rinsed and cut into
   ½-in coins
sea salt and freshly ground black pepper
2 tbsp olive oil
1 large egg
generous ¾ cup light cream
generous ¾ cup vegetable broth
2 garlic cloves, crushed
scant ½ cup soft goat cheese
generous ¼ cup grated Parmesan cheese
small handful of thyme leaves
1 eating apple
5¼oz ciabatta, torn into bite-size pieces
⅓ cup finely grated cheddar cheese

Serves: 4 | Takes: 1 hour 10 minutes

Preheat the oven to 350°F and butter a 8 x 12 x 2-in sheet pan.

Place the leeks in the pan, season generously with salt and pepper and toss with the olive oil. Dot the 1 tablespoon butter over the leeks, add a splash of water and cover tightly with foil. Bake for 30 minutes, shaking the pan occasionally.

Meanwhile, stir all the remaining ingredients, except the apple, ciabatta and cheddar, together in a jug.

When the leeks are done, peel, quarter and core the apple. Slice each quarter into the sheet pan. Add the ciabatta and toss to combine. Pour over the cream mixture and turn the bread to coat. Sprinkle over the cheddar and bake for another 30 minutes until golden. Serve immediately.

Crispy potato galettes with rosemary and garlic, and smoked salmon

This makes a glorious lunch, flanked by nothing more than a vibrant green salad. The key to this is slicing the potatoes very thinly—it's possible with a sharp knife but much easier on a mandoline or similar hand-held slicer.

3 tbsp goose or duck fat, or
   unsalted butter
1 fat garlic clove, crushed
14oz Charlotte or other waxy potatoes,
   ideally all a similar size
1 tsp chopped rosemary
sea salt flakes

To serve:
2 generous smoked salmon slices
2 tbsp crème fraîche

Serves: 2 | Takes: 1 hour

Preheat the oven to 425°F. Place the fat in a 8 x 12 x 2-in sheet pan and transfer to the oven for 2 minutes to melt. Pour the melted fat into a small bowl and stir in the garlic. Brush the residual fat in the pan all over the bottom so it's well covered.

Now make the galettes. Finely slice the potatoes with a mandoline or knife; slice and layer the potatoes in the sheet pan as you go to prevent the potatoes from discoloring. Closely overlap the slices to make a 5-in circle. Brush with the garlicky butter and sprinkle with rosemary and sea salt flakes. Continue layering—there should be enough potato for each galette to have three layers—until you have used up half the potatoes. Repeat to make a second galette. Brush the tops of the galettes with the melted garlic fat and roast for 30–40 minutes until cooked through and crisp at the edges.

Serve with curls of smoked salmon on top and a spoonful of crème fraîche.

Quick flatbread with spiced lamb and tahini

Even though you're making the dough from scratch, this is very easy and really doesn't take long. Serve with a simple salad of sliced red onion, soaked in water for 10 minutes and then drained, mixed with loads of chopped cilantro, lemon juice and extra virgin olive oil.

For the flatbread:
1 cup all-purpose flour, plus extra for dusting
½ tsp fine sea salt
½ tsp baking powder
1 scant tsp dried oregano
½ cup Greek yogurt

For the topping:
½ cup canned chopped tomatoes
2 tsp tomato paste
3 garlic cloves, crushed
2 tsp Aleppo or Turkish (or other) red pepper flakes
handful of chopped flat leaf parsley leaves and fine stalks
finely grated zest of ½ lemon
½ cup ground lamb
sea salt and freshly ground black pepper
4 tbsp tahini

Serves: 2–4 | Takes: 40 minutes

Preheat the oven to its highest setting. Line a 8 x 12 x 2-in sheet pan with foil so that it overhangs the short sides and place it in the hot oven.

For the flatbread, whisk the flour, salt, baking powder and oregano together in a mixing bowl. Gradually stir in the yogurt to make a rough dough. Work the dough with your hands to incorporate the flour at the bottom of the bowl. Knead on a lightly floured work surface for a few minutes until smooth. Cover with a damp cloth and leave to rest.

Meanwhile make the topping. Mix all the ingredients, except the tahini, together in a large bowl with a fork, breaking up the meat as much as possible, so everything is well amalgamated. Set aside.

Roll out the dough on a lightly floured surface to make a rectangle slightly smaller than the sheet pan. Carefully remove the hot pan from the oven and lay the dough inside. Spread the top with the tahini right up to the edges (loosen it with olive oil if necessary—it needs to be spreadable). Scatter the meat mixture over the top, spreading it out and breaking up clumps with a fork.

Bake for 12–15 minutes until the meat is browned and the bottom of the flatbread is slightly golden. Serve immediately.

Triple cheese and broccoli pasta

Here's the thing: this isn't an authentic Italian pasta dish but it doesn't pretend to be. It's just a very easy, super-delicious and hearty meal that's likely to become a favorite. It's worth stressing that fresh pasta—readily available these days in the chiller cabinet of convenience stores and supermarkets—is essential. The dried stuff won't work.

14oz fresh tagliatelle (from the chiller cabinet)
4¼oz broccoli, cut into tiny florets, thick stalks grated
⅓ cup soft goat cheese, Brie or blue cheese, chopped small
3½oz fresh mozzarella cheese, chopped small
⅓ cup finely grated Parmesan cheese, plus extra to serve

For the sauce:
1¼ cups whole milk
1¼ cups heavy cream
3 garlic cloves, crushed
sea salt and freshly ground black pepper

Serves: 4 | Takes: 25 minutes

Preheat the oven to 400°F.

Spread the pasta out in a 8 x 12 x 2-in sheet pan or oven dish, untangling any strands that are entwined or stuck together. Scatter over the broccoli and cheeses and toss well to combine.

Stir the sauce ingredients together with 3½ tbsp water and pour over the pasta. Using tongs, turn all the ingredients in the sauce so everything is coated; the pasta won't be submerged but that doesn't matter. Cover tightly with foil—use two layers if necessary to seal well.

Bake for 10 minutes. Remove from the oven and toss the pasta so everything gets a turn cooking in the cream. The pasta shouldn't look dry but if it does, add a splash of water. Cover tightly with the foil again and bake for a further 10 minutes. Serve immediately, with extra Parmesan on top.

Cheesy loaded potato skins with chorizo

Sometimes the most delicious things can be the most simple, and this is one of those: soothing, tasty and filling.

6 medium baking potatoes
3 tbsp sea salt flakes
2 tbsp unsalted butter
⅓ cup cream cheese
1½ cups grated cheddar cheese
3 scallions, finely sliced
sea salt and freshly ground black pepper
3oz cooking chorizo, chopped small

Serves: 6
Takes: about 1 hour 40 minutes

Preheat the oven to 425°F.

Wet the potatoes, shake off any excess water and sprinkle all over with the sea salt flakes. Place in a 8 x 12 x 2-in sheet pan and bake for 1–1 hour 15 minutes, or until completely cooked through and tender.

Brush the salt off the potatoes and cut in half lengthwise. Scoop the potato flesh into a bowl being careful not to split the skins. Add the butter, cream cheese and half the cheddar to the potatoes and mix until smoothish. Stir in the scallions and season with salt and pepper.

Fill the skins with the potato mixture and return to the sheet pan. Top each of the filled potato halves with chorizo and sprinkle over the remaining cheddar. Bake for a further 10–15 minutes, or until the cheese is bubbling. Serve immediately.

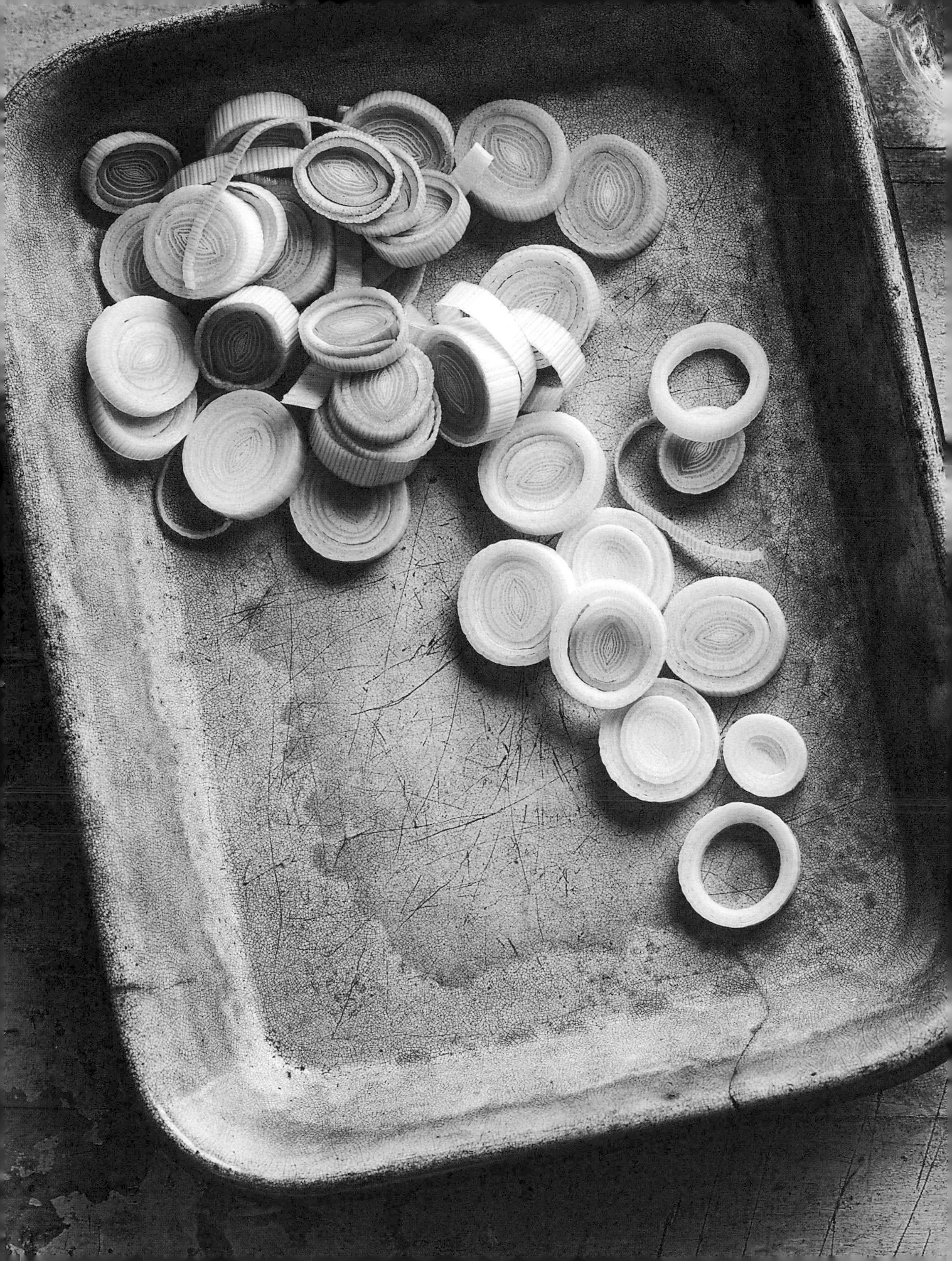

Dinner

Seafood, chorizo and potato stew with saffron

Pork and seafood are an ace combination and this quick dish is no exception. Salty, smoky, spicy chorizo pairs perfectly with sweet shrimp, mussels and clams, which release their briny juices as they steam. A chunk of bread to mop up the broth is the only extra you need.

7oz cooking chorizo, cut into ¾-in pieces
14oz new potatoes, cut into ¼-in slices
splash of olive oil
1⅔ cups fish broth (a good stock/ bouillon cube dissolved in boiling water is fine)
4 tbsp unsalted butter
½ tsp saffron strands, chopped
2 garlic cloves, crushed
1¼lb live mussels, rinsed and scrubbed
7oz raw king shrimp, weighed without heads or shells
1¼lb clams
½ cup dry white wine
sea salt and freshly ground black pepper
finely grated zest of ½ lemon
handful of chopped flat leaf parsley

Serves: 4 | Takes: about 45 minutes

Preheat the oven to 450°F.

Place the chorizo and potatoes in a 8 x 12 x 2-in sheet pan, toss with the olive oil and roast for 20 minutes until sizzling and the potatoes are tender.

Add the stock, butter, saffron, garlic, mussels, shrimp, clams and wine to the pan, season with salt and pepper and give it a little shake. Cover tightly with foil and roast for 12 minutes, or until the shrimp are pink and the mussels and clams have opened (discard any unopened ones). Serve immediately, sprinkled with lemon zest and parsley.

Salmon fillets with vine tomatoes, beans and green sauce

This is one of the best ways to cook salmon fillets—they're pretty much steamed, with just a few aromatics and vegetables. The green sauce is intense and punchy; perfect with fish, it's also fantastic spooned over lamb and chicken.

1½ cups cherry tomatoes, on the vine if possible
7oz green beans, trimmed
2 tbsp extra virgin olive oil
sea salt and freshly ground black pepper
4 salmon fillets, about 4½oz each and about 1¼in thick at thickest point
1 lemon
few dill sprigs (optional)

For the green sauce (optional):
2 tbsp capers, well rinsed
6 anchovy fillets
2 garlic cloves, crushed
⅔ cup flat leaf parsley leaves and fine stalks
1 cup basil leaves and fine stalks
2 shallots, roughly chopped
2 tbsp lemon juice
½ tsp Dijon mustard
½ cup extra virgin olive oil, or more if needed

Serves: 4 | Takes: 25 minutes

Preheat the oven to 425°F.

Place the tomatoes and beans in a 8 x 12 x 2-in sheet pan and pour over 1 tablespoon of the olive oil. Toss to coat and season generously with salt and pepper. Brush the salmon fillets on both sides with olive oil, season with salt and pepper, then add to the pan with the tomatoes and beans.

Thinly slice half the lemon, and arrange the slices on the fish. Squeeze the juice from the remaining lemon half over the fish and vegetables, and tuck in the dill. Cover tightly with foil and bake for 12 minutes, or until just cooked through. If the beans need a little more time, remove the fish and tomatoes from the pan and return to the oven for a few minutes.

Meanwhile, blitz the sauce ingredients together in a food processor until not quite smooth. Have a taste and add more lemon juice or pepper if needed—it shouldn't need any salt.

Serve the salmon with the sauce and vegetables.

Lamb loin with harissa and sweet potato mash

This dish has bags of flavor and looks like you've gone to a lot of trouble to make it, when actually it's a cinch. Just make sure you buy a good-quality jar of rose harissa paste.

2 thick lamb neck fillets, about 1¼lb in total
1 tsp sea salt flakes, plus extra for seasoning
freshly ground black pepper
2 heaped tbsp rose harissa paste
1¾lb sweet potato, peeled and cut into 1¼-in pieces
3 sage leaves or bay leaves
3 tbsp olive oil
3 garlic cloves, unpeeled
½ tsp ground cinnamon
½ tsp red pepper flakes
1 tbsp unsalted butter
bitter green salad, to serve (optional)

Serves: 4 | Takes: 1 hour

Pat the lamb dry with paper towels and season with salt and pepper. Rub all over with the harissa paste and set aside for at least 10 minutes.

Preheat the oven to 425°F.

Place the sweet potato, sage or bay leaves, olive oil, garlic, cinnamon, red pepper flakes, the 1 teaspoon of salt and 3 tablespoons of water in a 8 x 12 x 2-in sheet pan. Toss well with your hands so everything is combined and the sweet potato is coated in spiced oil. Add the butter to the pan and roast for 25 minutes, shaking the pan occasionally.

Push the sweet potato to one side—it should still fit in a single layer—and add the lamb. Roast for 12–15 minutes, turning the lamb over and shaking the pan halfway through. When done, it should still be springy to touch. Transfer to a plate, cover loosely with foil and leave to rest for 10 minutes.

Meanwhile, remove the sage or bay leaves and squeeze the garlic out of its papery skin into the pan with the sweet potato. Mash, incorporating all the meat juices from the pan, and season with more salt and pepper if needed.

Cut the lamb into thick slices and serve with the sweet potato mash, pouring any lamb juices from the plate over the meat. This is lovely served with a bitter green salad.

Roast hake with Parmesan crust, chorizo and sweet potatoes

Have your oven lovely and hot for this one so the crust turns crisp and golden. Keep an eye on the fish—thick fillets will need a little longer than thin ones, and you don't want to overcook them.

4 thick hake fillets (cod is also fine)
2 tbsp olive oil, plus extra for brushing
sea salt and freshly ground black pepper
1½lb sweet potatoes, cut into
    1¼-in chunks
about 2¼oz chorizo, finely sliced
2 large handfuls of spinach
1 lemon, cut into quarters

For the crust:
1 cup sourdough breadcrumbs
    (or similar)
⅓ cup grated Parmesan cheese
1 garlic clove, crushed
handful of flat leaf parsley leaves and
    fine stalks, finely chopped
finely grated zest ½ lemon
2 tbsp olive oil

Serves: 4 | Takes: 45 minutes

Preheat the oven to 425°F.

Lightly brush both sides of the fish with olive oil and season generously with salt and pepper. Set aside.

Place the sweet potatoes in a 8 x 12 x 2-in sheet pan, toss with the 2 tablespoons of olive oil and season generously with salt and pepper. Roast for 20 minutes, shaking the pan halfway through.

Meanwhile, toss all the ingredients for the crust together in a bowl.

When the sweet potatoes have had their 20 minutes, remove the pan from the oven and nestle the fish fillets into the pan, skin-side down if they have skin. Arrange a single layer of chorizo on top of each fillet, then cover with the crust mixture, pressing down gently to keep it in place. Roast for 10–15 minutes, or until the fish is just cooked through and the crust is golden.

Transfer the fish to warmed serving plates. Add the spinach to the sheet pan and toss with the sweet potatoes. The spinach should wilt slightly in the residual heat of the pan. Serve immediately with the fish, and lemon wedges for squeezing over the fish.

Sea bass with stewed summer vegetables

Roasting the vegetables brings out their gorgeous sweetness, and almost stews them into loveliness. Please be careful not to overcook the fish—it's criminal in a dish this delicious.

4 sea bass fillets
sea salt flakes and freshly ground
   black pepper
2 red onions, finely sliced
6 tbsp extra olive oil, plus extra
   if needed
2 tbsp unsalted butter
2 red bell peppers, finely sliced
12¼oz ripe tomatoes, roughly chopped
handful of black olives, halved
1 zucchini, about 8oz, halved lengthwise
   and sliced into half-moons
2 garlic cloves, crushed
handful of flat leaf parsley, chopped
1 tbsp dried oregano
3 tbsp balsamic vinegar
crusty bread, to serve

Serves: 4 | Takes: 1 hour 15 minutes

Preheat the oven to 400°F. Pat the fish dry with paper towels and season generously with salt and pepper. Set aside.

Spread the onions out in a 8 x 12 x 2-in sheet pan, toss with 3 tablespoons of the oil and season generously with salt and pepper. Roast for 10 minutes, shaking the pan halfway through.

Remove the pan from the oven and stir the butter into the onions until melted. Add all the remaining ingredients, including the remaining olive oil and more salt and pepper, but not the fish. Toss so everything is well combined.

Roast for 40 minutes, shaking the pan occasionally, until the vegetables are very tender and releasing their juices— if they look a little dry add a splash more olive oil.

Remove the pan from the oven, add the fish, skin-side up, and drizzle with olive oil. Roast for 8–10 minutes (the exact time will depend on the thickness of your fish) until just cooked through. Remove the skin from the fish and serve immediately with the vegetables spooned over, and crusty bread for dunking in the oily juices.

Veal parmigiana

This Italian classic is loved all over the world, and rightly so. Thin slices of breadcrumbed veal, layered up with tomato sauce, mozzarella and Parmesan, then baked, ticks all the boxes for a hearty, tasty feast. If you prefer, swap the veal for chicken breasts bashed thin between sheets of plastic wrap.

generous ¾ cup golden breadcrumbs
generous ¾ cup grated Parmesan cheese
generous ⅓ cup all-purpose flour
sea salt and freshly ground black pepper
1 large egg, lightly beaten
14oz high-welfare veal scallop, cut into
    4 equal pieces
oil, for brushing
1 cup canned chopped tomatoes
1 garlic clove, crushed
2 tsp dried marjoram
1 tbsp olive oil
½ tsp sea salt
¼ tsp granulated sugar
3½oz mozzarella balls, sliced
salad, to serve

Serves: 4 | Takes: 35 minutes

Preheat the oven to 425°F.

Combine the breadcrumbs and generous ¼ cup of the Parmesan in a shallow bowl. Put the flour in another bowl and season with salt and pepper. Place the beaten egg in a third shallow bowl.

Pat the veal dry with paper towels and season generously with salt and pepper. Coat both sides of the veal with the flour, then dip in the egg, then the breadcrumbs, pressing down so they stick. Set a wire rack over a 8 x 12 x 2-in sheet pan, lightly brush the rack with oil and place the crumbed scallops on top. Roast for 12 minutes, or until crisp on the outside and just cooked through.

Meanwhile, combine the tomatoes, garlic, marjoram, olive oil, the ½ teaspoon of sea salt, the sugar, and some pepper in a bowl.

Reduce the oven temperature to 350°F and carefully transfer the scallops from the rack to the sheet pan using a spatula. Cover each scallop generously with tomato sauce and top with the sliced mozzarella. Add more tomato sauce on top and sprinkle over the remaining Parmesan. Roast for 10 minutes, or until the cheese is melted and bubbling and the tomato sauce is hot. Serve immediately with salad.

Rare roast beef with hasselback potatoes and green beans

Like the chicken recipe on page 126, this is a complete roast meal for four people cooked in just one vessel: hooray for minimal cleaning up! The hasselback potatoes take a bit more effort than standard roasted potatoes, but they're worth it, as they soak up all the delicious juices from the beef.

3¼lb boned joint of beef (topside/round or sirloin)
1 tbsp mustard powder or finely ground mustard seeds
sea salt and freshly ground black pepper
3 tbsp dripping or lard
8 medium potatoes
8¾oz fine green beans, trimmed
splash of olive oil
squeeze of lemon juice

Serves: 4 | Takes: about 1 hour 20 minutes

Preheat the oven to 475°F.

Pat the beef dry with paper towels, and rub all over with the mustard and salt and pepper. Place in a 8 x 12 x 2-in sheet pan, add the fat or lard and roast for 15 minutes, basting halfway through.

Meanwhile, peel the potatoes, then cut slits, very close together, almost to the bottom, so the slices stay connected. The easiest way to do this is to sit a potato in the hollow of a wooden spoon—the edges of the spoon will prevent the knife from slicing all the way through.

Reduce the oven temperature to 350°F. Add the potatoes to the pan, spoon over lots of the hot fat and season generously with salt and pepper. Roast for 40 minutes, basting the beef and potatoes frequently—for medium-rare or medium roast for 5–10 minutes longer.

Meanwhile, toss the beans in the olive oil and some lemon juice and season with salt and pepper.

Remove the beef from the sheet pan and transfer to a plate. Cover loosely with foil and set aside. Nudge the potatoes to one side of the pan, add the beans (spread them out as much as possible) and return to the oven. Increase the oven temperature to 400°F and roast for 15 minutes, shaking the pan occasionally.

Carve the beef into thick slices and serve with the potatoes and beans, with the rested meat juices poured over.

Pork sausages with fennel, apples and red wine gravy

Apple is a perfect foil for the fatty sausages and rich wine gravy, and served with some green leaves, this makes a complete meal. Obviously it also goes beautifully with creamy mashed potato, so if you have some to hand then all the better.

8 large good-quality pork sausages
2 tbsp olive oil
1 large fennel bulb, trimmed, halved and
  thickly sliced (fronds reserved)
2 medium eating apples
sea salt and freshly ground black pepper
1¼ cups light red wine
4 tbsp chicken or vegetable stock
1½ tbsp balsamic vinegar
3 tbsp unsalted butter
1 tsp fennel seeds, crushed

Serves: 4 | Takes: 1 hour 15 minutes

Preheat the oven to 425°F.

Place the sausages in a 8 x 12 x 2-in sheet pan, toss with 1 tablespoon of the olive oil and roast for 20 minutes, shaking the pan halfway through. They should take on some lovely color.

Reduce the oven temperature to 350°F and add the sliced fennel to the pan. Core and quarter the apples, then cut into thick slices—there's no need to peel them—and add to the pan, too. Toss with the remaining oil—the pan will be crowded but that's fine, as everything will cook down a little. Season with salt and pepper and roast for a further 30 minutes.

Add the wine, stock, balsamic vinegar, butter and fennel seeds to the pan, season with salt and pepper and shake well. Roast for a further 15 minutes, or until the red wine has reduced a little and the gravy is bubbling nicely. Serve immediately, garnished with the reserved fennel fronds.

Pork belly with smoky beans

Pork belly is still a relatively inexpensive cut of meat that's soft and tender when cooked low and slow. Here the porky flavors melt into the beans to produce a dish that's insanely comforting and delicious. It does take a few hours to cook, but almost all of this is hands-off time in the oven.

3¼lb pork belly
2 x 14-oz cans cannellini or lima beans, drained
chopped flat leaf parsley, to serve

For the sauce:
1 onion, finely chopped
14oz canned chopped tomatoes
2 garlic cloves, crushed
2 tbsp tomato paste
5 tbsp apple cider vinegar
1 tbsp blackstrap molasses
2 tbsp smoked paprika
2 tsp English mustard powder
2 tsp chili powder
1 tsp fennel seeds
1 tsp ground cinnamon
3 tsp sea salt

Serves: 4 | Takes: 3 hours 15 minutes

Preheat the oven to 325°F.

Place all the sauce ingredients, including 3¼ cups just-boiled water, in a 8 x 12 x 2-in sheet pan and mix well. Place the pork belly on top, skin-side up. Spoon some of the liquid over the pork and rub into the skin. Cover loosely with foil and roast for 1½ hours.

Remove the foil, baste the pork with the sauce and roast, uncovered, for a further hour, adding water to the pan as needed to prevent the sauce drying out.

Stir the beans into the sauce, adding more water if too thick, and roast for a final 30 minutes. The beans should be cooking in a thick rich sauce.

When done, remove the skin from the pork, cut the meat into pieces and stir into the beans and sauce. Serve immediately, with chopped parsley.

Celery root, potato and anchovy gratin

Knobbly old celery root is a sadly undervalued root vegetable. It might not be photogenic, but it's absolutely delicious, with a sweet, nutty flavor reminiscent of the celery family of which it is a member. The anchovies add a gorgeous depth of flavour—no fishiness at all.

1⅔ cups milk, plus extra if needed
1⅔ cups heavy cream
2 garlic cloves, crushed
3 anchovy fillets, very finely chopped
2–3 thyme sprigs
freshly ground black pepper
10½oz celery root
10½oz waxy potatoes
scant 1 cup grated Comté cheese
green salad, to serve (optional)

For the topping:
3½oz sourdough or country-style
   bread, torn into small pieces
2 tbsp olive oil
scant ½ cup grated Parmesan cheese

Serves: 4 | Takes: about 1 hour,
   plus 5 minutes cooling

Preheat the oven to 375°F. Combine the milk, cream, garlic, anchovies and thyme in a 8 x 12 x 2 in sheet pan and season with pepper.

Peel and very finely slice the celery root and potatoes, ideally on a mandoline, adding the vegetables to the creamy pan liquid as you go to prevent them browning. Bake for 20 minutes, shaking the pan halfway through. Add a little more milk if necessary so the vegetables are just submerged.

Meanwhile, mix all the topping ingredients together in a bowl. Set aside.

When the vegetables have had their 20 minutes, sprinkle over the Comté, then the topping mix. Bake for a further 30 minutes—the vegetables should be beautifully tender when the time is up. Leave to cool in the pan for 5 minutes before serving—a green salad is the perfect accompaniment.

Spiced vegetables and garbanzo beans with yogurt

Curry powder sometimes raises eyebrows among purists but there's nothing wrong with a shortcut now and then, as long as you layer other flavors into the dish. Seek out a good-quality hot curry powder and you won't look back.

6 tbsp rapeseed oil or other flavorless oil, plus extra if needed
1 medium eggplant, about 10½oz
½ tsp fine sea salt
2 medium onions, roughly chopped
10½oz cauliflower florets, cut small
sea salt and freshly ground black pepper
4 garlic cloves, crushed
1 heaped tsp grated fresh ginger
2–3 tbsp good-quality hot curry powder
2 x 14-oz cans chopped tomatoes
14-oz can garbanzo beans (not drained)
2 tsp sea salt flakes

To serve:
squeeze of lemon juice
1 cup Greek yogurt
large handful of chopped mint

Serves: 4 generously | Takes: 1 hour 20 minutes, includes 20 minutes draining

Preheat the oven to 425°F. Pour the oil into a 8 x 12 x 2-in sheet pan and place inside the oven to heat.

Meanwhile, chop the eggplant into ¾-in cubes, place in a colander and toss with the ½ teaspoon of salt. Set the colander over a bowl or sink to drain for 20 minutes. Spread the eggplant out on paper towels, pat dry and squeeze out any excess moisture.

Carefully place the onions, eggplant and cauliflower into the hot oil in the sheet pan, season with salt and pepper and toss to coat. Roast for 20–25 minutes, shaking the pan occasionally, or until the vegetables are almost tender and a little browned at the edges.

Add the garlic, ginger and curry powder to the pan and mix in well, adding a little more oil to moisten the spices if too dry. Return the pan to the oven for 5 minutes.

Add the chopped tomatoes, the garbanzo beans with the can water, and the sea salt flakes to the pan and stir. Return to the oven for 30 minutes, stirring once or twice, or until the sauce is bubbling and slightly reduced, and the vegetables and garbanzo beans are very tender.

Serve with a squeeze of lemon, a spoonful of yogurt on top and a generous sprinkling of mint.

Chicken thighs with creamy leek and caper sauce

The sauce here is a gorgeous one, with the rich and creamy notes lifted by the sharp saltiness of the capers. It really does make you wonder why anything is cooked on the stove.

8 chicken thighs, skin on
1lb new potatoes, halved
  (or quartered if large)
2 tbsp olive oil
sea salt and freshly ground black pepper
⅔ cup heavy cream
7 tbsp dry vermouth (Noilly Prat is
  great) or white wine
1 tsp bouillon powder
2 garlic cloves, crushed
1 large leek, finely sliced
3 tbsp capers
2 handfuls of watercress

Serves: 4–6 | Takes: about 1 hour

Preheat the oven to 425°F.

Place the chicken and potatoes in a 8 x 12 x 2-in sheet pan and toss with the olive oil. Arrange the chicken skin-side up and season generously with salt and pepper. Roast for 25 minutes until the skin is crisp and starting to turn golden.

Meanwhile, combine all the remaining ingredients, except the watercress, with 7 tbsp boiling water in a jug, then season with salt and pepper. When the cooking time for the chicken and potatoes is up, pour the creamy mixture into the pan, then turn the chicken in the liquid to coat but return the chicken to skin-side up.

Roast for a further 30 minutes until the chicken is cooked through and the sauce is bubbling. Serve with the watercress scattered on top.

Oven "fried" buttermilk chicken with corn and greens

The highlight of this Southern-inspired feast is the chicken: it's ridiculously tender, juicy and tasty thanks to its lengthy bath in a buttermilk marinade. It really does make all the difference.

8 chicken drumsticks, skin removed
generous 1 cup panko breadcrumbs
4 tbsp golden breadcrumbs
1 tsp paprika
1 tsp cayenne pepper
½ tsp fine sea salt
1 tsp garlic powder
olive oil, for drizzling and brushing
4 small corn cobs, or 2 cobs cut in half
2 tbsp unsalted butter
½ tsp smoked paprika
sea salt and freshly ground black pepper
2⅔ cups sliced collard greens

For the marinade:
2 tbsp lemon juice
1 cup plus 1 tbsp buttermilk or
    natural yogurt
2 garlic cloves, crushed
2 tsp Dijon mustard
½ tsp dried oregano
½ tsp sea salt
¼ tsp freshly ground black pepper

Serves: 4 | Takes: 55 minutes, plus at
    least 2 hours marinating

Mix all the marinade ingredients together in a large zip-lock bag. Add the chicken and squelch the contents to ensure the chicken is completely coated in the marinade. Refrigerate for at least 2 hours, or ideally overnight. Remove from the fridge 30 minutes before cooking.

Preheat the oven to 400°F.

Mix both breadcrumbs, the paprika, cayenne, salt and garlic powder together in a shallow bowl. Shake any excess marinade off the chicken and dredge in the breadcrumb mixture, pressing down to ensure the coating sticks. Transfer to a lightly oiled wire rack as you go.

Spread each of the cobs with one-quarter of the butter and sprinkle with a pinch of smoked paprika and salt and pepper. Wrap tightly in foil. Place in a 8 x 12 x 2-in sheet pan. Sit the rack bearing the chicken over the pan and transfer to the oven. Roast for about 35 minutes until the chicken is cooked through and the coating is crisp.

Meanwhile, toss the greens with a splash of olive oil and season with salt and pepper. Five minutes before the chicken has finished cooking, push the corn to one side and add the greens to the sheet pan. Push the chicken to one side so that it sits over the corn, not the greens (the steam tends to make the coating go soggy) and cook for the final 5 minutes. Serve immediately.

Duck breasts with juniper, blackberry and port sauce

Dark, rich and a little gamey, duck breast is gorgeous paired with blackberries in a mellow port sauce. The skin does not turn quite as crisp as it does when cooked the conventional way, seared first in a skillet on the stove, but it is delicious nonetheless.

2 boneless duck breasts, skin on
10 juniper berries, crushed
½ tsp sea salt flakes
3 garlic cloves, unpeeled and bashed
small bunch of thyme
salad or greens, to serve (optional)

For the sauce:
5 tbsp port
⅔ cup beef broth
2½ tbsp light brown soft sugar
2 tbsp unsalted butter
generous 1 cup blackberries

Serves: 2 | Takes: 35–40 minutes

Preheat the oven to 475°F and place a 8 x 12 x 2-in sheet pan inside on the highest rack to heat.

Pat the duck dry with paper towels and score the skin diagonally with a sharp knife. Using a pestle, bash the juniper berries with the salt in a mortar, then rub the mixture into the duck skin.

When the oven has reached the correct temperature, quickly place the duck breasts, skin-side down, in the hot pan and roast for 5 minutes.

Reduce the oven temperature to 400°F, turn the duck breasts over and baste with the rendered fat. Add the garlic and thyme to the pan, shake well and roast for a further 10 minutes, basting halfway through.

Transfer the duck to a plate and cover loosely with foil. Tip out all but 2 tablespoons of the fat from the pan. Stir in the port, stock, sugar and butter. Add the blackberries and squash them a bit with a fork. Return to the oven for 12 minutes—the mixture should thicken slightly.

Remove and discard the thyme sprigs. Squeeze out the garlic flesh and discard the skins. Mash the berries and garlic with a fork and amalgamate into the sauce, adding in any juices from the duck plate.

Serve the duck in slices with the sauce spooned over. Some new potatoes and salad or greens would be lovely alongside.

Risotto with smoked mackerel, peas and lemon

Smoked mackerel is a rich and incredibly tasty oily fish, and it's widely available, which really makes this dish a winner.

1 tbsp olive oil
2 tbsp unsalted butter
1 small onion, grated
1 fat garlic clove, crushed
1⅔ cups risotto rice
3⅓ cups fish broth (good-quality stock cube or bouillon is fine), plus a splash extra if needed
3½ tbsp dry sherry (dry vermouth or white wine also works well)
1 tsp hot smoked paprika
½ tsp sea salt
2 smoked mackerel fillets, skin removed and flaked
½ cup frozen peas
3 tbsp crème fraîche
finely grated zest of ½ lemon and lemon juice, to taste
2 tbsp chopped dill

Preheat the oven to 400°F.

Place the olive oil and butter in a 8 x 12 x 2-in sheet pan and transfer to the oven for 2–3 minutes to melt. Add the onion and garlic, toss well to coat in the oil and bake for 5 minutes to soften.

Add the rice to the pan, stir to coat in the buttery oil, then add the stock, sherry, paprika and salt. Cover tightly with foil and bake for 15 minutes.

Stir in the mackerel, peas and crème fraîche. Add a splash more stock if the rice is looking a little dry, recover with foil and bake for a further 5 minutes. Stir in the lemon zest and juice (to taste) and dill and serve immediately.

Serves: 2–4 | Takes: 30 minutes

Beef and chile meatballs

It is a truth universally acknowledged that you can never have too many meatballs, so this recipe makes enough for six hungry meatball-lovers. Alternatively, they make fantastic canapés—just transfer to a platter with the sauce, spear the balls with toothpicks and pass around.

extra virgin olive oil, for brushing
2¼lb ground beef
1 tbsp red pepper flakes
1 tbsp smoked paprika
1 tbsp nigella seeds
2 tsp ground cumin
2 garlic cloves, crushed
2 large eggs, lightly beaten
1 cup soft breadcrumbs
generous 1 cup grated Parmesan cheese
sea salt flakes and freshly ground
   black pepper
1lb 10oz strained tomatoes
½ tsp granulated sugar

Makes: 40 balls | Takes 45 minutes

Preheat the oven to 425°F and brush a 8 x 12 x 2-in sheet pan with olive oil.

Place all the ingredients, except half the Parmesan, all the strained tomatoes and sugar, in a mixing bowl. Mix well with your hands until everything is beautifully combined. Season well with salt and pepper.

Using damp hands, roll the mixture into golf ball-sized balls (roughly 1oz each) and transfer to the prepared sheet pan. They will be quite snug, so place them close together. Brush with olive oil and roast for 20 minutes.

Mix the strained tomatoes and sugar together, then pour over the meatballs and season well with salt and pepper. Sprinkle over the remaining Parmesan.

Bake for a further 15 minutes until the sauce is bubbling and the meatballs are cooked through. Serve immediately.

Roast chicken dinner with apple and pistachio stuffing

Fact: there is no easier way to cook a roast chicken dinner with all the trimmings than this. Roasting the bird directly on the oven rack allows all the delicious chicken juices to fall through to the vegetables below. And there are even greens and gravy.

1 medium free-range chicken, about 3¼lb
rapeseed oil, for drizzling
sea salt and freshly ground black pepper
10½oz small carrots
1½lb potatoes, ideally Maris Piper or Yukon Gold
2 cups finely sliced cavolo nero, tough stems removed
generous ¾ cup hot chicken broth

For the stuffing:
1 medium eating apple, peeled, cored and diced very small
1⅓ cups breadcrumbs, ideally from a sourdough or good-quality, country-style loaf
⅓ cup pistachio nuts, roughly chopped
1 large egg, lightly beaten
2 garlic cloves, crushed
1 tsp fennel seeds, crushed in a mortar
grated zest ½ lemon

Serves: 4 | Time: 1 hour 30 minutes

Preheat the oven to 475°F. Set the oven rack on the middle shelf and another underneath, leaving just enough space between to fit a 8 x 12 x 2-in sheet pan.

Mix all the stuffing ingredients together and stuff into the chicken's cavity. Pat the chicken dry with paper towels. Drizzle over some oil, sprinkle generously with salt and pepper, then rub into the skin. Place the bird on the top rack and slot the oven tray on the shelf underneath so it can catch the fat from the bird. Roast for 15 minutes.

Meanwhile, cut any carrots bigger than the width of your thumb in half or quarters lengthways. Peel the potatoes and cut into quarters, or eighths if very large, ideally no larger than 2in wide. When the chicken has had its 15 minutes, reduce the oven temperature to 400°F. Add the vegetables to the pan and turn them in the hot fat; add a little more oil if necessary to lightly coat, and season generously with salt and pepper. Place the pan directly underneath the chicken again and roast for 50 minutes, shaking the pan occasionally.

Add the cavolo nero to the pan, pour over half the stock and gently turn the vegetables so the kale is coated in the liquid and sitting among the potatoes and carrots, not on top. Roast for 10 minutes.

Transfer the chicken and vegetables to serving plates. Pour the remaining stock into the pan, stir to incorporate the juices and caramelized bits to make a light gravy. Spoon over the chicken and vegetables and serve immediately.

Saffron rice with chicken, seafood and sherry

Purists would have a field day if this dish were ever called paella—so let's not speak of it. Suffice to say this is "inspired" by that classic dish and uses lots of Spanish flavors to produce a hearty and deeply flavorsome rice feast.

4 chicken thighs, skin on
olive oil, for drizzling
sea salt and freshly ground black pepper
1 large red onion, chopped
1 red bell pepper, seeded and chopped
3 garlic cloves, crushed
4½ cups chicken broth
2 tbsp dry sherry
2 ripe tomatoes, peeled and diced
1 tbsp smoked paprika
1 bay leaf
pinch of saffron strands, finely chopped
generous 2 cups paella rice
⅔ cup frozen peas
8 raw king shrimp, peeled and heads removed (optional)
3½oz squid rings
lemon wedges, to serve

Serves: 4 | Takes: 1 hour 10 minutes

Preheat the oven to 400°F.

Place the chicken in a 8 x 12 x 2-in sheet pan, skin-side up, drizzle over a little olive oil and season with salt and pepper. Roast for 25 minutes until the skin is golden. Remove from the pan and set aside.

Discard all but 2 tablespoons of fat from the pan. Add the onion, pepper and garlic, toss to coat and roast for 10 minutes until softened.

Pour in the broth and stir to scrape up any caramelized bits on the bottom. Add the sherry, tomatoes, paprika, bay leaf, saffron, rice and lots of salt and pepper. Stir well, then return the chicken to the pan. Cover tightly with foil and bake for 25 minutes, by which time the chicken should be cooked through.

Add the peas, shrimp and squid to the pan, poking them into the rice. There should still be some liquid left to be absorbed, but if not add a splash more stock or water. Cover with foil and roast for a final 5 minutes—the shrimp should be pink and the squid tender and cooked through. Serve immediately with lemon wedges.

Sweet Things

Roast apricots with cardamom, spiced cream and amaretti

This simple dessert is packed with flavor: apricots dripping with cardamom-infused honey, spiced cream and crunchy amaretti cookies. You could make it all in advance and just assemble when needed.

12 ripe apricots, halved and pitted
4 long strips unwaxed lemon peel
12 green cardamom pods, crushed and seeds removed
6 tbsp honey
2 cups heavy cream
1 heaped tbsp powdered sugar, sifted
1 tsp ground cinnamon
4 amaretti cookies, crushed

Serves: 4 | Takes: 30 minutes, plus cooling

Preheat the oven to 375°F.

Place the apricots, cut-side up, in a single layer in a 8 x 12 x 2-in sheet pan and tuck the lemon peel between them.

Using a mortar and pestle, finely grind the cardamom seeds. Mix the cardamom together with the honey and ½ cup warm water. Pour the mixture over the apricots, making sure to fill indentations in the fruit. Bake for about 20 minutes, basting occasionally. The fruit should be very tender but still holding its shape. Leave to cool to room temperature.

Very lightly whip the cream—it should flop off the spoon readily—and fold in the powdered sugar and cinnamon.

To assemble, layer the apricots and cream into four serving glasses and top with the crushed amaretti, or simply arrange on plates. Serve immediately.

Peanut butter caramel brownies

These are very rich and chocolatey, their sweetness tempered by the lovely savory note of peanuts—basically, they're the ultimate sheet pan treat.

vegetable oil, or other flavourless oil, for brushing
12oz caramel sauce, from a can or jar
⅓ cup smooth or crunchy peanut butter, ideally no added sugar
1 cup minus 1½ Tbsp all-purpose flour
¾ cup unsweetened cocoa powder
generous pinch of salt
½ tsp baking powder
1 cup unsalted butter, softened
1⅔ cups unrefined granulated sugar
3 large eggs
1 tsp vanilla extract
1¼ cups semisweet chocolate chips

Makes: 12 generous squares
Takes: 1 hour

Preheat the oven to 350°F. Line a 8 x 12 x 2-in sheet pan with baking parchment, letting it overhang the sides, and lightly brush with oil.

Stir the caramel and peanut butter together to make a smooth, pouring consistency. Set aside.

Whisk the flour, cocoa powder, salt and baking powder together in a bowl.

Beat the butter and sugar together with electric beaters or an electric mixer until fluffy. Gradually beat in the eggs, then the vanilla extract. Stir in the flour mixture to make a very thick batter, then fold in the chocolate chips.

Add half the peanut butter caramel to the batter and semi-mix it in—you want to retain some visible swirls. Spread out evenly in the prepared pan, then pour the remaining peanut butter caramel on top.

Bake for about 25 minutes, or until firm to touch. The caramel itself might be a bit gooey but will firm up as it cools. Leave in the pan for 10 minutes then use the foil to lift the brownies out onto a cutting board. When cool, cut into 12 large squares.

Polenta slices with blackberries and apple

This is a slab of gorgeousness: tender chunks of apple in a buttery, lemony cake and studded with juicy berries. It can make a lovely dessert served with lightly whipped cream. Or pack it for a picnic.

1 cup plus 2 tbsp unsalted butter, softened, plus extra for greasing
scant 1⅔ cups ground almonds
1 cup fine polenta/cornmeal or semolina (it must be finely ground)
scant 1¼ cups self-rising flour
2 tsp baking powder
pinch of salt
generous 1⅓ cups unrefined granulated sugar
4 large eggs, lightly beaten
finely grated zest and juice of 2 lemons
12oz eating apples
3 tbsp milk
generous 1 cup blackberries

Makes: 12 large slices
Takes: 50 minutes

Preheat the oven to 350°F. Line a 8 x 12 x 2-in sheet pan with foil so that it overhangs the sides. You will probably need to use two sheets, one lengthwise and one crosswise. Butter the foil well.

Whisk the almonds, polenta or semolina, flour, baking powder and salt together in a bowl and set aside. Beat the butter and sugar together in another bowl, ideally with electric beater until light and fluffy. Slowly beat in the eggs and lemon zest.

Peel, core and chop the apples into ¼-in cubes, transferring to a bowl and tossing with a little of the lemon juice as you go to prevent them discoloring.

Gradually stir the flour mixture into the eggs and butter mixture, alternating with the lemon juice and milk, to make a smooth batter. Fold in the apples.

Scrape the mixture into the prepared pan and smooth the top with a spatula. Press the blackberries into the top, pushing them down well.

Bake for 30 minutes until a skewer pushed into the center comes out clean. Cool in the pan, then cut into 12 large squares.

Raspberry jam tart cookies

These are an addictive cross between a tart and a cookie—hence the name. But whatever you call them, the tender, buttery pastry filled with toasted hazelnuts and slicked with raspberry jam is quite irresistible.

1 cup blanched hazelnuts
1 cup unsalted butter, plus extra
    for the pan if needed
2 cups plus 2 tbsp all-purpose flour,
    plus extra for dusting
1 tsp mixed spice
½ tsp fine sea salt
1 cup granulated sugar
1 large egg
1 vanilla bean, split in half lengthwise
    and seeds scraped out
¾ cup raspberry jam, at room
    temperature

Makes: 12 | Takes: 1 hour

Preheat the oven to 350°F.

Place the hazelnuts in a 8 x 12 x 2-in sheet pan. Roast for up to 10 minutes, or until golden, shaking the pan halfway through—keep an eye on them so they don't burn. Cool for a few minutes, then blitz in a food processor until finely ground. Set side to cool completely.

Meanwhile, line the sheet pan with baking parchment so it overhangs the sides; a few dabs of butter in the pan will help to keep it in place, if needed. Tip the cooled nuts into a mixing bowl, add the flour, mixed spice and salt and whisk together. Set aside.

Beat the butter and sugar together with electric beaters or an electric mixer until fluffy, then beat in the egg and vanilla seeds. Gradually stir the flour mixture into the butter mixture to make a soft dough. Set aside about 12oz, or roughly one-third, of the mixture for the topping, and spoon the rest into the prepared sheet pan in mounds. Using lightly floured hands, firmly press the mounds into an even layer of dough covering the base of the pan.

Stir the jam to loosen, then spread over the dough with the back of a spoon. Scatter clumps of the remaining dough on top and flatten with the back of a lightly floured spoon. There should be jam visible through gaps in the topping.

Bake for 30 minutes, or until pale gold on top. Leave to cool in the pan for 10 minutes, then carefully lift out using the baking parchment for handles. Transfer to a wire rack to cool completely, then cut into 12 rectangles.

Peach and plum pie with vanilla and almonds

In some places this kind of pie is known as a slab pie. This might reflect the way it looks, which admittedly isn't fancy. Let's call it a relaxed pie instead. Or rustic. Whatever, it's delicious.

2 sheets of ready-rolled shortcrust pastry, about 14 x 9in each
1¾lb mixed peaches and plums, ripe but firm
⅓ cup granulated sugar
1 tbsp cornstarch
1 vanilla bean, split in half lengthwise and seeds scraped out
3 tbsp ground almonds
1 large egg, lightly beaten
2 tsp raw brown sugar
pouring cream or ice cream, to serve

Serves: 6–8 | Takes: 1 hour 10 minutes

Preheat the oven to 350°F. Line a 8 x 12 x 2-in sheet pan with baking parchment so it overhangs the sides. Place one of the pastry sheets in the pan—it will be too big, but arrange it so the excess comes up the sides. Chill in the fridge until needed.

Halve, stone and thinly slice the peaches and plums, leaving the skin on. Place in a mixing bowl, add the sugar, cornstarch and vanilla seeds and stir to combine. Set aside for 5 minutes, then stir again—the fruit should be coated in thick sugary juices.

Meanwhile, trim the second pastry sheet to a 8 x 12-in rectangle.

Sprinkle the ground almonds over the pastry base in the sheet pan, leaving a ¾-in border. Arrange the fruit on top. Place the trimmed pastry sheet over the fruit and brush the edges with beaten egg. Fold the edges of the bottom pastry sheet up and over the top pastry sheet and press together to seal. You should have a shallow rectangular pastry package. Make several slits in the top to let out the steam, brush with egg and sprinkle with brown sugar.

Bake for 40–45 minutes until burnished on top and golden underneath. Serve with pouring cream or ice cream.

(Pictured overleaf)

Orange and caraway slices with orange blossom glaze

This cake is basic in a way, but the combination of orange and caraway is slightly unusual and the flavor is amazing. The simple orange glaze on top is all it needs.

¾ cup plus 2 tbsp unsalted butter, softened, plus extra for greasing
scant 1¼ cups all-purpose flour
⅔ cup spelt flour
1 tsp baking powder
generous pinch of fine sea salt
1 cup minus 1½ tbsp light brown soft sugar
3 large eggs, lightly beaten
finely grated zest and juice of 2 oranges
2 tsp caraway seeds, pounded in a mortar or ground in a spice grinder

For the glaze:
1½ cups powdered sugar, sifted
splash of orange blossom water or orange juice
finely grated zest of 1 orange
3 tbsp milk

Makes: 12 slices | Takes: 45 minutes

Preheat the oven to 350°F. Butter a 8 x 12 x 2-in sheet pan and line with baking parchment.

Combine the flours, baking powder and salt together in a bowl.

Beat the butter and sugar together with electric beaters or an electric mixer until fluffy. Gradually beat in the eggs, then the orange zest and caraway seeds.

Stir the butter mixture into the flour mixture, alternating with the orange juice, to make a thickish batter. Scrape into the prepared sheet pan, making it as level as you can, and smooth the top with a spatula. Bake for 20 minutes, or until firm to the touch. Leave in the pan for 5 minutes, then turn out on a wire rack to cool.

Meanwhile, combine all the glaze ingredients in a small bowl. When the cake is completely cold, spread the glaze over the top, leave to set and cut into 12 portions.

Strawberry and rhubarb brioche pudding

This is old-fashioned "bread and butter pudding" really, made posh with brioche and a secret layer of baked fruit. Awesome.

unsalted butter for greasing
2 cups strawberries, hulled and halved
10½oz rhubarb, cut into 1¼-in pieces
½ cup granulated sugar
1 tbsp cornstarch
4 large eggs
1⅔ cups heavy cream
1⅔ cups milk
1 vanilla bean, split in half lengthwise
    and seeds scraped out
grated zest of 1 orange
1 large brioche loaf, cut into
    ½-in slices

Serves: 8 | Takes: 1 hour 20 minutes

Preheat the oven to 325°F and lightly butter a 8 x 12 x 2-in sheet pan or dish.

Place the strawberries and rhubarb in the prepared pan, sprinkle over 1½oz of the sugar and the cornstarch and toss to coat.

Mix the eggs, cream, milk, the remaining sugar, the vanilla seeds and orange zest together in a jug.

Working one slice at a time, dip the brioche into the cream mixture until thoroughly soaked and arrange on top of the fruit, slightly overlapping. Pour any of the remaining mixture over the top, and set aside for 15 minutes while the bread soaks.

Bake for 40–45 minutes, or until puffed and golden.

Rye gingerbread cake

Intensely gingery and fragrant, this cake is equally nice served with a cup of tea as it is eaten warm from the oven with a scoop of vanilla ice cream for dessert. The rye flour adds an extra flavor note to the scale, but it's fine to substitute with wheat flour if you don't have any to hand.

1½ cups all-purpose flour
scant ½ cup rye flour
½ tsp ground cinnamon
1 tsp ground ginger
1 tsp baking soda
¼ tsp fine sea salt
½ cup unsalted butter, cut into
    very small pieces
½ cup light corn syrup
½ cup blackstrap molasses
6 tbsp syrup from a jar of preserved
    ginger
1 large egg, lightly beaten
3½oz chopped preserved ginger
    from a jar

Serves: 12 | Takes: 35 minutes

Preheat the oven to 350°F. Line a 8 x 12 x 2-in sheet pan with baking parchment—you want it to come up and over the sides, so lightly butter the pan first to keep the paper in place.

Whisk the flours, spices, baking soda and salt together in a mixing bowl.

Place the butter in a separate bowl or jug, add 7 tbsp just-boiled water and stir until melted. Add the corn syrup, molasses and ginger syrup, then stir in the egg.

Whisk the wet ingredients into the dry to make a smooth batter, then fold in the chopped preserved ginger. Pour into the prepared sheet pan, making sure the batter is evenly spread out.

Bake for about 20 minutes, or until firm to the touch and an inserted skewer comes out clean. Leave in the sheet pan for a few minutes, then lift out onto a wire rack to cool using the overhanging baking parchment as handles.

Baked apple dumplings with blueberry and fennel seed crumble

Baked apples are gorgeous, but stuffed with fruity crumble and wrapped in a blanket of puff pastry, they're even better. This dish is extremely simple and definitely looks fancier than it is trouble to make.

2 x sheets of ready-rolled puff pastry, about 11oz each
all-purpose flour, for dusting
4 Braeburn, Granny Smith or other eating apples, about 3½in in diameter
1 large egg, lightly beaten
1 tbsp raw brown sugar, for sprinkling
cream or vanilla ice cream, to serve

For the filling:
4 tbsp rolled oats
3 tbsp dried blueberries (any other dried fruit is fine, chopped if large)
3 tbsp unsalted butter, softened
generous pinch of fine sea salt
2 tbsp maple syrup, plus extra to serve (optional)
2 tbsp chopped toasted hazelnuts
1 tsp fennel seeds

Serves: 4 | Takes: 1 hour

Preheat the oven to 400°F and line a 8 x 12 x 2-in sheet pan with baking parchment.

Roll out the pastry sheets on a lightly floured work surface so they are a little thinner than they come in the packet. Using a plate as a guide, cut out two 8-in disks from each pastry sheet. Refrigerate until needed.

Mix all the filling ingredients together in a bowl.

Peel the apples, then remove most of the core with a small knife or apple corer. Don't cut through to the bottom—you want to leave a little apple so the filling doesn't fall through. Use a teaspoon or melon baller to widen the hole. Tightly pack the apples with the filling—it doesn't matter if some of the filling pokes over the top.

Sit one of the apples on a pastry disk and lightly moisten around the edge with water. Gather the pastry up over the apple, pleating it as you go. Pinch the pastry at the top to seal, then trim off any excess. Repeat with the remaining apples and pastry, transferring each one to the prepared sheet pan as you go.

Brush the pastry with the beaten egg and sprinkle with the brown sugar. Bake for 40–50 minutes, or until the pastry is puffed and golden and the apples are cooked through; an inserted skewer should go through easily. Serve hot, with cream or vanilla ice cream, drizzled with extra maple syrup, if you like.

Magic melting mocha cake

This is wickedly good: an airy chocolate cake atop a hidden lake of not-too-sweet chocolate sauce spiked with espresso. Make sure you have a bowl of cold, lightly whipped cream to serve with this, or a stash of vanilla ice cream.

⅔ cup unsalted butter, cut into pieces
scant 2½ cups self-rising flour
1½ tsp baking powder
1 cup light muscovado sugar
¾ cup unsweetened cocoa powder
1 cup milk
4 large eggs
whipped cream or vanilla ice cream,
    to serve

For the topping:
7 tbsp light muscovado sugar
scant ⅔ cup unsweetened cocoa powder
3½ tbsp espresso coffee

Serves: 8 | Takes: 50 minutes

Place the butter in a 8 x 12 x 2-in sheet pan. Preheat the oven to 325°F and while it reaches temperature place the pan inside for the butter to melt.

Meanwhile, whisk together the flour, baking powder, sugar and cocoa together in a mixing bowl.

When the butter has melted, pour into a jug and set aside to cool for a few minutes. Meanwhile, brush the pan with the residual butter so all the sides are coated.

Add the milk and eggs to the melted and cooled butter and mix well. Stir this into the dry ingredients to make a smooth batter. Scrape into the buttered sheet pan and smooth the top with a spatula.

Mix all the topping ingredients together with 2 cups just-boiled water and pour over the batter. Bake for about 30 minutes until the top is firm: there will be a pool of sauce under the cake. Serve hot topped with whipped cream or ice cream.

(Pictured overleaf)

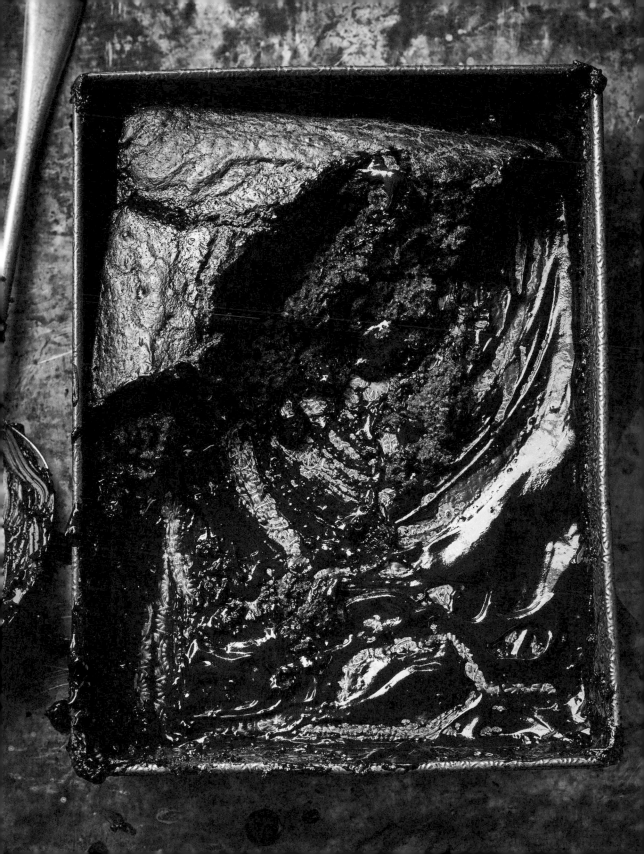

Roast pears in Marsala and saffron syrup

This simple but sumptuous dessert appeals to all the senses: it tastes and looks wonderful, and your kitchen will smell ambrosial while it's cooking. The grown-up flavors—alcohol, herbs and fruit—really sing together beautifully.

3 tbsp unsalted butter, cut into small pieces
½ cup light brown soft sugar
generous pinch of saffron strands, chopped
generous ¾ cup sweet Marsala or medium sherry
2 tbsp lemon juice
1 rosemary sprig
4 firm but ripe pears
generous ¾ cup mascarpone cheese
generous ¾ cup crème fraîche
2 tbsp powdered sugar, sifted
1 vanilla bean, split in half lengthwise and seeds scraped out
toasted slivered almonds, to serve (optional)

Serves: 4 | Takes: 1 hour

Preheat the oven to 400°F.

Place the butter, sugar and saffron in a 8 x 12 x 2-in sheet pan and pour over ½ cup just-boiled water. Stir to dissolve the sugar and melt the butter—it doesn't matter if there are still traces left. Stir in the Marsala and lemon juice, and add the rosemary sprig.

Peel and halve each pear, then scoop out the core with a teaspoon or melon baller. Transfer the fruit, cut-side down, to the sheet pan as you go, spooning over some of the liquid to stop it discoloring.

Roast for about 50 minutes, basting frequently, and gently turning the fruit over halfway through. When done, the pears should be very tender and the liquid reduced to lovely amber syrup.

Meanwhile, lightly whisk the mascarpone, crème fraîche, powdered sugar and vanilla seeds together in a bowl. Refrigerate until needed.

Serve the pears with the syrup spooned over and topped with the mascarpone cream and slivered almonds, if you like.

Apple and almond tart with thyme

Fruity, buttery and fragrant with vanilla and thyme, this is a chic but very simple dessert inspired by the French classic *tarte fine aux pommes*. A scoop of vanilla ice cream or cloud of sweetened whipped cream (spiked with Calvados if you're feeling fancy) would be perfect on the side.

1 sheet of all-butter puff pastry, about 10½oz
½ cup ground almonds
2½ tbsp granulated sugar
1 vanilla bean, split in half lengthwise and seeds scraped out
¼ tsp ground cinnamon
4 eating apples, about 14oz
squeeze of lemon juice
2 tsp raw brown sugar
1 tbsp unsalted butter
few thyme sprigs

Serves: 4–6 | Takes: 40 minutes, plus 20 minutes chilling

Preheat the oven to 400°F and line a 8 x 12 x 2-in sheet pan with baking parchment.

Trim the pastry into a 8 x 12-in rectangle and transfer to the prepared pan. Mark out a ½-in border with the back of a knife and prick the area inside the border all over with a fork.

Mix the almonds, granulated sugar, vanilla seeds and cinnamon together in a small bowl. Break up any clumps of vanilla seeds by rubbing them between your fingers, as for butter into flour. Sprinkle evenly inside the pastry border. Refrigerate for at least 20 minutes.

Working quickly, peel, quarter and core the apples, then finely slice them, ideally on a mandoline. Transfer to a bowl as you go, tossing with a little lemon juice to prevent discoloration.

Tightly arrange overlapping apple slices in rows within the pastry border—if you're feeling artistic, place them all facing the same way, like fish scales. Sprinkle over the brown sugar, then dot with tiny pieces of the butter. Arrange the thyme sprigs on top and bake for 25 minutes, or until puffed and golden.

Coconut rice pudding with cardamom and kirsch cherries

Most countries have their own version of rice pudding, and this has a bit of a Scandinavian vibe, with the inclusion of cardamom, a favorite Nordic spice. It's a great dessert but also does nicely for breakfast if there's any left over.

2 tbsp unsalted butter, chopped into pieces, plus extra for greasing
14-oz can coconut milk
5½ cups whole milk, or more if needed
1 cup pudding rice or other short-grain rice
¼ cup unrefined granulated sugar
3 cardamom pods, crushed with the side of a knife
3 short strips of lemon zest
pinch of sea salt
1 whole nutmeg, grated
1 can or jar of black cherries in kirsch syrup (any kind of nonalcoholic syrup is also fine)

Serves: 6 | Takes: 1 hour 40 minutes

Preheat the oven to 300°F and generously butter a 8 x 12 x 2-in sheet pan or oven dish.

Pour both the milks into the prepared sheet pan and stir well, breaking up any thick blobs of coconut milk with the back of a spoon. Stir in all the remaining ingredients, except the cherries.

Bake for 1½ hours, stirring halfway through, until the rice is tender and creamy. Add a splash more milk if the rice threatens to dry out before it's cooked.

Remove the cardamom pods before serving with the black cherries and syrup spooned over.

index